PUTTING THE PIECES BACK TOGETHER AFTER
Adultery

31 DAYS OF PRAYER & RESTORATION FOR WOMEN

GINA ERWIN

Inspired Grace Media Productions Llc.

Lexington, Kentucky

Putting the Pieces Back Together After Adultery: 31 Days of Prayer & Restoration for Women

Copyright 2018 by Gina Erwin

Published in the United States by Inspired Grace Media Productions.

www.igmproductions.com

All Rights Reserved.

This book or parts thereof may not be reproduced in any form, stored in a retrieval system, or transmitted in any form by any means - electronic, mechanical, photocopy, recording, or otherwise - without prior written permission of the publisher, except as provided by The United States of America Copyright Law.

All Scripture quotations are taken from the Holy Bible, New International Version. Copyright 1973, 1978, 1984, 2011 by Biblica, Inc. The "NIV," "New International Version," is trademark registered in the United States Patent and Trademark Office by Biblica, Inc.

The author has made every effort to provide accurate information based on their personal experiences.

Contributing Author: Gina Erwin

Photograph Courtesy of: Gina Erwin

Cover Design: Rebecca Garcia, Dark Wish Designs

Interior Layout/Graphic Design: Rebecca Garcia, Dark Wish Designs

PAPERBACK ISBN: 978-0692127179

Printed in the United States of America

First Edition Special Sales Most Inspired Grace Media books are available at special quantity discounts when purchased in bulk by corporations, organizations, and special-interest groups. For information, please email info@igmproductions.com

Dedications

To GOD
This book is dedicated 1st and foremost to God for without Him I would be nothing. He gives me the strength and wisdom to move forward and continue when times are dark, and storms are raging in my life. God is my everything, above and beyond all things. I thank Him for guiding me and giving me the wisdom and knowledge to use my experiences to help others.

To Aunty/Mommy Yetta
You have been with me from birth, every step of my journey. You have loved me unconditionally and always held me up when I was going down. Your wisdom and guidance have motivated me to hold onto God and strive to be the best person I can be. The day my mother died, you stepped up and stepped in and have maintained the role every day thereafter. I love and appreciate all you have done and been for me. I thank God for you. I love you past the heavens and back.

To All My Mommies That Loved & Guided Me
Ruth Fortune, Phyllis Smalls, Elizabeth Ervin, Thelma Tate, Pastor Myrtle Carlton, and my birth Mother Lillian Erwin. Each of these women played a vital role in my upbringing and knowledge of the greatness of God. I Love each of you.

To My Children ~ Malik, Georgina, & Gillian
You are my reasons to be the best I can be. Although you believe I am superwoman, I am not and my experience with adultery showed each of you that I need you just as much as you need me. I want you to be better than me and go further than I ever will. I love each of you with all my heart and will love you forever and even after. Each of you will always be my babies even though you may be grown. It is my prerogative.

To My Sister and Friend Charis
God placed you in my life. This I have no doubts about. You are not a leaf or a branch to my tree, you are one of my roots. You prayed over me as I stumbled through my storm. You were the voice of reason when I believed, no reason existed. Your family became my family and you became my sister in Christ. You motivated me to not just go on, but to walk in God's purpose for me. You motivated me to write and do so many things. You had more faith in me and my abilities than I ever could. I thank God for you my sister and look forward to all the remarkable things God will have us doing together in the future. I love you so much. Thank you, Sis!

To All My Sisters, Brothers, Friends & Family
There are too many of you to name but you know who you are. Thank you for all your love and support. It is much appreciated. I love you all.

A Special Thank You to Wendy ~ My Cousin & Friend
You have always supported me and made me feel like I could do whatever I put my mind to. You jumped right in and was ready to use your skills to aid me in making my first book a success. I love and appreciate you and all you do.

Daniel 3:17

"If we are thrown into the blazing furnace, the God we serve is able to deliver us from it, and he will deliver us!"

Table of Contents

Dedications 1
Introduction 11
Day One 14
    Connecting with God 14
    Scriptures 15
    Prayer 16
My Journal 17
Day Two 18
    Building A Relationship with God 18
    Scriptures 20
    Prayer 21
My Journal 22
Day Three 23
    Trusting God 23
    Scriptures 25
    Prayer 26
My Journal 27
Day Four 28
    The Revealing 28
    Scriptures 29
    Prayer 30
My Journal 31
Day Five 32
    Knowing & Acting Accordingly 32
    Scriptures 33
    Prayer 35

    Scriptures 36

    Prayer 37

My Journal 38

Day Six 39

    Misconception #1: God is punishing me. He let this happen to me.

    Scriptures 41

    Prayer 42

    Scriptures 43

    Prayer 44

My Journal 45

Day Seven 46

    Misconception #2: It is her fault. She went after my husband. 46

    Scriptures 48

    Prayer 49

My Journal 50

Day Eight 51

    Misconception #3: My mate did this on purpose. He wanted to hurt me. 51

    Scriptures 53

    Prayer 54

My Journal 55

Day Nine 56

    Misconception #4: It is my fault. I did something wrong. 56

    Scriptures 57

    Prayer 58

My Journal 59

Day Ten 60

 Misconception #5: The best way to overcome this is to find me another man 60

  Scriptures 62

  Prayer 64

My Journal.. 65

Day Eleven 66

 Misconception #6: I will be fine. This will not affect me. 66

  Scriptures 68

  Prayer 70

My Journal.. 71

Day Twelve 72

 Misconception #7: I am damaged. No one will want me and/or another man's children 72

  Scriptures 74

  Prayer 76

My Journal.. 77

Day Thirteen... 78

 Misconception #8: I cannot go on 78

  Scriptures 80

  Prayer 82

My Journal.. 83

Day Fourteen.. 84

 Acknowledgement.. 84

  Scriptures 85

  Prayer 86

My Journal.. 87

Day Fifteen 88

Discerning the Situation	88
Scriptures	90
Prayer	92
My Journal	93
Day Sixteen	94
Discerning Your Inner Circle	94
Scriptures	94
Prayer	97
My Journal	98
Day Seventeen	99
Discern What You Listen To	99
Scriptures	101
Prayer	102
My Journal	103
Day Eighteen	104
Comprehending Physically	104
Scriptures	105
Prayer	106
My Journal	107
Day Nineteen	108
Comprehending Mentally	108
Scriptures	110
Prayer	111
My Journal	112
Day Twenty	113
Comprehending Spiritually	113
Scriptures	114

Prayer	116
My Journal	117
Day Twenty-One	118
Comprehending Financially	118
Scriptures	119
Prayer	120
My Journal	121
Day Twenty-Two	122
Comprehending Sexually	122
Scriptures	123
Prayer	124
My Journal	125
Day Twenty-Three	126
Dealing with Your Emotions	126
Scriptures	127
Prayer	130
My Journal	131
Day Twenty-Four	132
Self-Forgiveness	132
Scriptures	134
Prayer	136
My Journal	137
Day Twenty-Five	138
Forgiveness of All Individuals Involved	138
Scriptures	140
Prayer	142
My Journal	143

Day Twenty-Six 144
    Forgiveness of Your Mate 144
    Scriptures 146
    Prayer 148
My Journal 149
Day Twenty-Seven 150
    Decision-Making 150
    Scriptures 151
    Prayer 153
My Journal 154
Day Twenty-Eight 155
    Healing (Letting It Go) 155
    Scriptures 156
    Prayer 158
My Journal 159
Day Twenty-Nine 160
    The Rollercoaster Ride Realization 160
    Scriptures 161
    Prayer 162
My Journal 163
Day Thirty 164
    Moving Forward 164
    Scriptures 165
    Prayer 169
My Journal 170
Day Thirty-one 171
    Turning Tests into Testimonies & Pain into Purpose 171

Scriptures 173
Prayer 176
My Journal 177
Conclusion 178
Bible Verse that Inspired the Book 180
Affirmation Statement 182
About the Author 183
Contact Gina here; 184
Coming Soon from Gina Erwin 185

Introduction

Marriage is a sacred union between a husband, a wife, and God. To stay on the right path both parties must give 100% and trust God to do the rest. Some people say marriage is 50~50. However, being imperfect, even giving all your effort is not enough. That is where God comes in and fills the cracks. Outside of our love for each other, God's will and guidance and our trusting in Him totally are what is needed for our marriages to survive. We must communicate with God daily and pray for guidance and wisdom. As we are all imperfect, we will make mistakes. We must get back up, ask God and those we hurt for forgiveness and move forward doing better to withstand temptation.

Almost, every woman has experienced adultery in some form or fashion in their lives. Adultery is an emotional, stressful, inconvenient situation to go through. It is viewed differently by each woman experiencing it. Some women easily deal with it, forgive, and move forward with their significant other. Some live with it daily, just allowing it to take place. Others deal with it head on and fight back and others experience a total devastation. For some it is a mistake on the part of their partner and after it is dealt with personally in private or through counseling some can move on without problem. Some women feel that it is their lack that causes it and allows it to continue. Other women experience betrayal, hurt, unbelief, broken hearts, and even total devastation.

I know because I personally have dealt with adultery. I am ashamed to admit I committed adultery. Although it happened because I was given the attention and affection that I was lacking in my relationship, it was still wrong on my part.

I was also a casualty of adultery. It hurt me to my core. I was on the verge of giving up because I did not want to deal with the situation and the pain that came along with it. Through the grace of God, the love of my children, choice friends and family members, I gained the ability to get myself together and trust God to get me through.

Experiencing adultery from both sides has given me a lot of insight, especially when it comes to understanding, blaming, and forgiveness. I felt the best thing to do was to use my experience to help others going through and getting past the effects of adultery.

As hurtful as adultery is, most people do not set out to commit adultery or at the very least get caught. Our fleshly bodies desire things and people that we are not meant to connect with on that level, but it happens and if we do not stay aware of our personal needs, wants, emotions, and feelings, we will find ourselves being tempted and falling for that temptation.

As a victim of adultery, you will face many choices and decisions that will live on after you make the choices. You need to be in the right state of mind to make the correct choices and decisions. It is easy to act out of anger and difficult to act out of pure Godly love. However, as a child of God, He expects you to act according to His will. This is also essential for you to get back on the path that God has planned for you. You must control the situation, not let it control you.

No two adulterous situations are the same and neither are their outcomes. What is right for some is not necessarily right for all. No matter which end of the spectrum you are on there is one common denominator that each of us share, God. "With God, all things are possible" (Matthew 19:26) and that includes overcoming the effects of adultery.

God is a guiding force and His word, (the holy bible), gives everyone a manual to follow to get through any and everything including adultery. This 30~day prayer recovery is to help you in turning to and trusting God to guide you to where He wants you to be.

This 30~Day Prayer Recovery starts at the beginning of the adultery process. You may be in the beginning, somewhere in the middle, or at the end stages. No matter where you are, I feel starting at the beginning will allow you to see things you may have missed throughout all you have gone through, so it is beneficial to go through each of the 31 days to get the full benefit of the book. There may be a message or something God wants you to reflect on that you bypassed.

Each day there is a reading section on a specific topic of the stages of adultery. Read and reflect on your place with the topic. Look up scriptures that follow as well. Next there is a prayer of the day to align you with God and allow Him to guide you. I purposely made the prayers different lengths to show there is no specific way to pray. Prayer is a conversation with God and can be as long or short as you make it. Lastly, there is a "My Journal" page for you to write down your thoughts, reflections, and feelings. Writing your thoughts and rereading them later is a great reflection tool that can be used to see yourself for who you are. Writing also gives you a starting point to see where you are at and what you need to do to move forward in God's will and purpose for your life.

My prayer is that each of you reading this book receive a word from God, guidance from Him, a roadmap to get you where God wants you to be, and total healing. Trust God and let Him get you through. "Cast your cares on the Lord and he will sustain you; he will never let the righteous be shaken" (Psalm 55:22).

Day One

Connecting with God

You may be asking, what does this have to do with the adulterous situation I am going through? Let me tell you. God is the Alpha and the Omega (the beginning and end) of all things. For things to work out for your best, God must be the central part of it. All things work for the good of God and benefit your purpose in life.

The number 3 represents completeness and the Trinity (Father, Son, and Holy Spirit). So, for the first 3 days of this prayer recovery, we will focus on God, opening yourself up to Him, and allowing Him in to be your guiding force now and forever.

You may be blaming God for your current situation, wondering why He allowed this to happen to you, crying out to Him, or just leaving Him out of it and trying to handle it on your own. No matter which place you are at, you need God.

For this our first day of prayer recovery we are going to tell God what we are feeling. God knows our every thought already, but He wants and desires you to communicate with Him through prayer.

Scriptures

"I am the Alpha and the Omega" says the Lord God, "who is, and who was, and who is to come, the Almighty". ~ **Revelations 1:8 NIV**

"And we know that in all things God works for the good of those who love Him, who have been called according to His purpose. For those God foreknew he also predestined to be conformed to the image of His Son, that he might be the firstborn among many brothers and sisters. And those he predestined, he also called; those he called, he also justified; those he justified, he also glorified". ~ **Romans 8:28-30 NIV**

"Take notice, you senseless ones among the people; you fools, when will you become wise? Does he who fashioned the ear not hear? Does he who formed the eye not see?
Does he who disciplines nations not punish? Does he who teaches mankind lack knowledge? The Lord knows all human plans; He knows that they are futile. ~ **Psalm 94:8-11 NIV**

Gina Erwin

Prayer

Dear God,

Today, I come to You openly and profess that I feel **(state your feelings)**. I know I cannot get through this without You. I thank You for loving me and showing me mercy and grace. While I may not know why I am going through this, I know You know all things, including the outcome of this situation. God motivate me to read your word and follow through daily with this prayer recovery program. I ask You to open my heart, mind, body, and soul to You so that I can hear, feel, see, taste, and smell You and what I need to. Move me to allow You to guide and inform me of the truth that will set me free. Without You nothing exists including me. I need You God and I give myself to You and your will. I love You God. Thank You for who and all that You are.

In Jesus' Name
Amen

Putting the Pieces Back Together After Divorce

Date: _____

_____
_____
_____
_____
_____
_____
_____
_____
_____
_____
_____
_____
_____

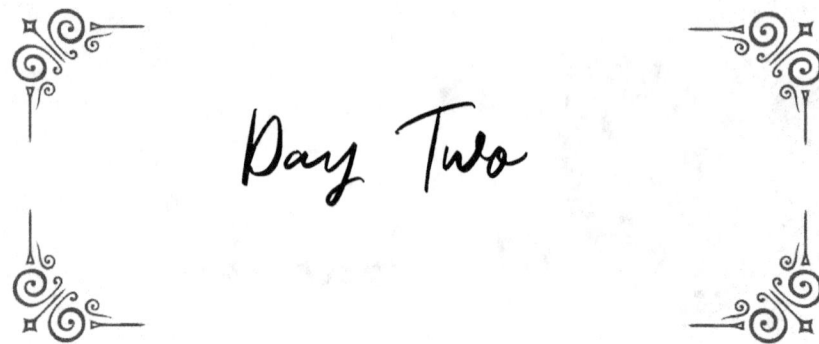

Day Two

Building A Relationship with God

Now that you have talked to God and submitted yourself to Him, it is time to build on that relationship. How do you do that? The simple answer is to build your schedule around God, not find time in your schedule for God. We all have responsibilities. There is school, work, family, and personal things we must address every day. When we attempt to find time to read the bible and pray, we can lose track of time, forget, get sidetracked, or just not find the time. To prevent this, our schedule must be built around God.

A relationship with God requires reading His word (the Holy Bible), studying His word, applying His principles to our lives, and praying (daily communication with God). As you read this some of you are already wondering where you will find the time to do these things. What is the first thing you do when you wake up? Try praying and talking to God before you do anything else. Thank Him for waking you up. Ask Him to help you with all you must do today.

Do you sit at the table and have breakfast or coffee? Do you ride a train, bus, or are you a passenger in a vehicle (not driving)? Read a scripture during these times. The bible comes in audio format that you can play in your vehicle if you are driving. You do not have to read for hours, just read a few scriptures, just one chapter. The point here is to begin reading or listening to the bible daily. Once you get into a pattern it will come naturally. If you can or have the time you can read or listen for longer periods of time.

Studying the bible takes more time and concentration. Studying means you read the word, understand the context and meaning, see how it can be applied in your life, and make changes accordingly. Some people go to church for bible study. That is good, but you need to also study God's word on your own. There are many personal lessons to be learned.

At bedtime once everything is quiet, is a wonderful time to pray. You can thank God for all He has done for you and talk to Him about your concerns and fears. Ask God to guide your steps and actions.

Find or create a quiet place, even if it is in a closet or small room. Honestly, sometimes I go in the bathroom and just sit in a chair and talk to God. It needs to be somewhere that you can avoid distractions and focus on God and talking to Him.

You are going through an emotional experience and you desperately need God to get through. "God is love" (1 John 4:8). His love will give you the strength, knowledge, wisdom, and ability to get through this. He is there waiting for you with open arms. Talk to Him, trust Him, and love Him as He loves you.

P.U.S.H. ~ **P**ray **U**ntil **S**omething **H**appens.

Scriptures

"Ask and it will be given to you; seek and you will find; knock and the door will be opened to you. For everyone who asks receives; the one who seeks finds; and to the one who knocks, the door will be opened. Which of you, if your son asks for bread, will give Him a stone? Or if he asks for a fish, will give Him a snake? If you, then, though you are evil, know how to give good gifts to your children, how much more will your Father in heaven give good gifts to those who ask Him! So, in everything, do to others what you would have them do to you, for this sums up the Law and the Prophets". ~ **Matthew 7:7-12**

"Dear friends, let us love one another, for love comes from God. Everyone who loves has been born of God and knows God. Whoever does not love does not know God, because God is love. This is how God showed His love among us: He sent His one and only Son into the world that we might live through Him. This is love: not that we loved God, but that he loved us and sent His Son as an atoning sacrifice for our sins. Dear friends, since God so loved us, we also ought to love one another. No one has ever seen God; but if we love one another, God lives in us and His love is made complete in us. ~ **1 John 4:7-12 NIV**

Putting the Pieces Back Together After Divorce

Prayer

Dear God,

I come before You to first thank You for all You have done in my life. Now in my life, I am **(distraught, upset, emotional, hurt, etc. use your feelings here)**. I need You God. Please help me to build a strong relationship with You and draw closer to You. Help me to get through all that I am going through. Help me to see the path You have set before me and what I need to do to travel down your planned road. God please give me wisdom and insight into You and all that I need to know to have a strong binding relationship with You. I know your love is unconditional and will be a protection for me. Help me to keep You first and plan everything else around You. God, I love You and I need You now and forever!

In the Mighty Name of Jesus, I Pray
Amen

Gina Erwin

My Journal

Date: _____

_____
_____
_____
_____
_____
_____
_____
_____
_____
_____
_____
_____

Day Three

Trusting God

You have begun this book and have been reading scriptures and praying. Now it is time for the big step ~ trusting God. Some of you may already trust God and some of you may trust Him some, but now we are going to see what total trust in God is all about.

If we trust in God, He will fix every situation. He is our creator and He knows what we need before we do. Sometimes we think we need some things or some people in our lives and we try to hold onto what God is trying to remove for our own good. Trusting in God is the natural way to success. If you are doing what God requires of you, He will provide you with everything you need. It may not happen overnight, but it will happen when God says so.

What we ask for may not always come in the way we think it should, but your needs will be provided in the manner God sees fit. We must remember God knows the future and what we may see as a need not being fulfilled, may just be God protecting us from danger.

God works in the spirit because He is a spirit. We must learn through prayer and bible study to worship Him in spirit and truth.

If we truly trust God with our whole hearts and minds, we do not fear or worry. We know He is there, and He will provide. He will make things work out for our good, even if it does not look like it right now.

Gina Erwin

Give all your problems to God and have faith that He will take care of you and your needs.

Scriptures

"Trust in the Lord with all your heart and lean not on your own understanding; in all your ways submit to Him, and he will make your paths straight". ~ **Proverbs 3:5-6 NIV**

"Therefore, I tell you, do not worry about your life, what you will eat or drink; or about your body, what you will wear. Is not life more than food, and the body more than clothes? Look at the birds of the air; they do not sow or reap or store away in barns, and yet your heavenly Father feeds them. Are you not much more valuable than they? Can any one of you by worrying add a single hour to your life? And why do you worry about clothes? See how the flowers of the field grow. They do not labor or spin. Yet I tell you that not even Solomon in all His splendor was dressed like one of these. If that is how God clothes the grass of the field, which is here today and tomorrow is thrown into the fire, will he not much more clothe you—you of little faith? So, do not worry, saying, 'What shall we eat?' or 'What shall we drink?' or 'What shall we wear?' For the pagans run after all these things, and your heavenly Father knows that you need them. But seek first His kingdom and His righteousness, and all these things will be given to you as well. Therefore, do not worry about tomorrow, for tomorrow will worry about itself. Each day has enough trouble of its own". ~ **Matthew 6:25-34 NIV**

Yet a time is coming and has now come when the true worshipers will worship the Father in the Spirit and in truth, for they are the kind of worshipers the Father seeks. God is spirit, and His worshipers must worship in the Spirit and in truth". ~ **John 4:2324 NIV**

"And we know that in all things God works for the good of those who love Him, who have been called according to His purpose". ~ **Romans 8:28 NIV**

Prayer

Dear God,

I am **(confused, hurt, scared, etc. use your feelings here)**. I am desiring to let go and allow You to manage my woes. God, I do not know what to do. I am **(State your fears and worries)**. I need your help. Please provide for my needs and remove my fears. Build my faith in You. Strengthen me and my faith in times of turmoil such as this. I try to do it all and fix it all and I cannot. Help me see and know You are there for me and will never leave me or hurt me. God, I love you!

In the Mighty Name of Jesus
Amen

Putting the Pieces Back Together After Divorce

Date: _____

_____

_____
_____
_____
_____
_____

_____
_____
_____

_____
_____
_____
_____

Day Four

The Revealing

Adultery is revealed most times by accident. However, some women have an inkling or intuitive feeling that something is not quite right within their relationship. They feel that something is wrong, and something is going on. You may be the woman that directly asks your partner, the one that starts checking phones, emails, social media sites, and other communication sources for information, or the one that just stands and waits to see what happens next. Whichever role you take on, today, we are going to consult the ultimate source and information provider, God.

Before you pray and ask God to reveal the truth, know that you are mentally prepared to handle it. When you pray and ask God to reveal to you what you need to know, He will at the right time and in the manner best for your situation. He may reveal it at once or in time. God is a God of order, not messiness. God will work it towards what is best for you.

Once the truth is out, there is no turning back. You will have to deal with it. How you deal with it is your choice. However, you should deal with it in a manner pleasing to God and in line with His principles.

Scriptures

"Remind the people to be subject to rulers and authorities, to be obedient, to be ready to do whatever is good, to slander no one, to be peaceable and considerate, and always to be gentle toward everyone". ~ **Titus 3:1-2**

"Our people must learn to devote themselves to doing what is good, in order to provide for urgent needs and not live unproductive lives". ~ **Titus 3:14**

"For God is not a God of disorder but of peace—as in all the congregations of the Lord's people". ~ **1 Corinthians 14:33**

"But I tell you, love your enemies and pray for those who persecute you", ~ **Matthew 5:44**

Gina Erwin

Prayer

Dear Father in Heaven,

I feel something is wrong in my relationship. I need to know what is going on and what I should do. God please reveal what I need to know and give me the strength to deal with it. Give me the wisdom to remain calm and react in a manner proper to your will.
God if nothing is wrong, then make it clear and show me the reason. I am feeling this way. With You God I can get through anything. Stay with me and hold me close. Allow me to know all I need to.
Thank You for a spirit of discernment and for strengthening me as I go forward doing my best to please You.

In Jesus' Name
Amen

My Journal

Date: _____

_____
_____
_____
_____
_____
_____
_____
_____
_____
_____
_____
_____

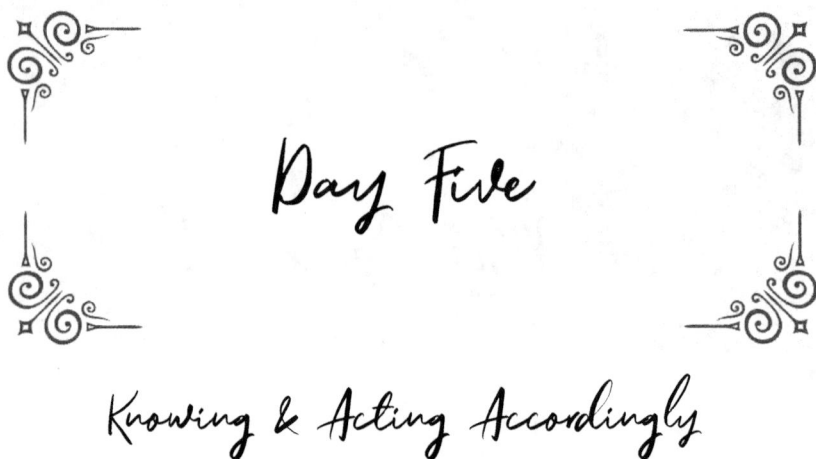

Day Five

Knowing & Acting Accordingly

Now that you are aware of the situation, you need to be aware of your actions and in control of your thoughts. Adultery especially causes us to act out of the norm because it affects the heart and is something meaningful to your life and your future. When unexpected and difficult situations arise, it is easy to allow your thoughts to go wild and act before thinking about what you are doing. You want to know why and more than likely your first desire is revenge.

You may be feeling mental and physical pain and be crying out to God for help. You may want to go after the other woman. You may feel like you cannot go on. You may want to turn to drugs, alcohol, or some other substance to help you forget for the moment. None of these are the answer. No matter what you are feeling, you must stop and pray. Ask God for wisdom and to help you deal with what you are feeling. This will prevent you from making the wrong choices and doing something you will regret later. As bad as this situation is, you must respond in a Godly manner. Two wrongs do not make a right.

Once you have gotten yourself somewhat together and under control, you need to know what is real and what is not. There are many misconceptions when it comes to adultery. The next few days we are going to look at these misconceptions to help you make the best choices for yourself and everyone else concerned.

Scriptures

"Do not conform to the pattern of this world but be transformed by the renewing of your mind. Then you will be able to test and approve what God's will is - His good, pleasing and perfect will". ~ **Romans 12:2**

"In your anger do not sin: Do not let the sun go down while you are still angry, and do not give the devil a foothold. Anyone who has been stealing must steal no longer, but must work, doing something useful with their own hands, that they may have something to share with those in need. Do not let any unwholesome talk come out of your mouths, but only what is helpful for building others up according to their needs, that it may benefit those who listen. And do not grieve the Holy Spirit of God, with whom you were sealed for the day of redemption. Get rid of all bitterness, rage and anger, brawling, and slander, along with every form of malice. Be kind and compassionate to one another, forgiving each other, just as in Christ God forgave you". ~ **Ephesians 4:26-32**

"My son, if you accept my words and store up my commands within you, turning your ear to wisdom and applying your heart to understanding - indeed, if you call out for insight and cry aloud for understanding, and if you look for it as for silver and search for it as for hidden treasure, then you will understand the fear of the Lord and find the knowledge of God. For the Lord gives wisdom; from His mouth come knowledge and understanding. He holds success in store for the upright, he is a shield to those whose walk is blameless, for he guards the course of the just and protects the way of His faithful ones. Then you will understand what is right and just and fair - every good path. For wisdom will enter your heart, and knowledge will be pleasant to your soul. Discretion will protect you, and understanding will guard you. Wisdom will save you from the ways of wicked men, from men whose words are perverse, who have left the straight paths to walk in dark ways, who delight in doing wrong and rejoice in the perverseness of evil, whose paths are crooked and who are devious in their ways." ~ **Proverbs 2:1-15**

"The acts of the flesh are obvious: sexual immorality, impurity and debauchery; idolatry and witchcraft; hatred, discord, jealousy, fits of rage, selfish ambition, dissensions, factions and envy; drunkenness, orgies, and the like. I warn you, as I did before, that those who live like this will not inherit the kingdom of God. But the fruit of the Spirit is love, joy, peace, forbearance, kindness, goodness, faithfulness, gentleness, and self-control. Against such things there is no law. Those who belong to Christ Jesus have crucified the flesh with its passions and desires. Since we live by the Spirit, let us keep in step with the Spirit. Let us not become conceited, provoking and envying each other". ~ **Galatians 5:19-26**

Putting the Pieces Back Together After Divorce

Prayer

Dear God,

I am feeling **(State your feelings)**. I need You to help me stay in control. I want to **(State your desires good and bad)**. I need You to strengthen and guide me. God, please guide my steps and order my thoughts. I know this is not going to be easy, but with your help and guidance, I will prevail. Help me God please.
Thank You for all You do and all You will do to help me get through this.

In Jesus' Name
Amen

Scriptures

"Remind the people to be subject to rulers and authorities, to be obedient, to be ready to do whatever is good, to slander no one, to be peaceable and considerate, and always to be gentle toward everyone". ~ **Titus 3:1-2**

"Our people must learn to devote themselves to doing what is good, in order to provide for urgent needs and not live unproductive lives". ~ **Titus 3:14**

"For God is not a God of disorder but of peace—as in all the congregations of the Lord's people". ~ **1 Corinthians 14:33**
"But I tell you, love your enemies and pray for those who persecute you", ~ **Matthew 5:44**

Prayer

Dear Father in Heaven,

I feel something is wrong in my relationship. I need to know what is going on and what I should do. God please reveal what I need to know and give me the strength to deal with it. Give me the wisdom to remain calm and react in a manner proper to your will.

God if nothing is wrong, then make it clear and show me the reason. I am feeling this way. With You God I can get through anything. Stay with me and hold me close. Allow me to know all I need to.

Thank You for a spirit of discernment and for strengthening me as I go forward doing my best to please You.

In Jesus' Name
Amen

My Journal

Date: _____

Day Six

Misconception #1: God is punishing me, He let this happen to me.

Blaming God is often one of the first things some of us do. After all, He is in control is He not? God is our creator. He created us out of love, and He loves us. He created us to love and to be loved. He is not a puppeteer, sitting on the throne, pulling strings to make us do things or allowing things to hurt us. When Adam and Eve ate the fruit from the tree of knowledge, sin was not the only thing that entered the world. Freewill also entered. While God has a set plan for our lives, the fact that we have freewill detours us from the path He planned for us. If we stay in tune with God and follow His will, we will ultimately complete the path He has planned for us. Freewill however allows us to make right and wrong decisions that will detour us from that path. Freewill allows us to go through trials, tests, hardships, tribulations, and detours of our own making.

The devil also places traps and hardships in our paths to detour us from God's plan. He does not want us to be obedient to God and fulfill the purpose and plan God has for our lives. The devil told God we only obey Him and are faithful to Him because of what He does for us. This is the reason the devil can place detours in our path and try His best to keep us from pleasing God. However, not all trials, tribulations, tests, hardships, and detours come from the devil. Our actions lead to some as well. However, these hardships can be overcome whether they originate from the devil or our own actions. God will help and guide you through all these things if you trust in Him and follow His will.

Did God place this man in your life? Did He choose this man for you, or was it your freewill choice? Did you consult God in prayer? Were you and your mate evenly or unevenly yoked? Were you running on love or lust? Did you place your trust in this man and not in God? Did you place this man before God in your life? Did you commit adultery in your past? I am not in any way saying that it is your fault. Even if you did not do anything wrong and was totally in accord with God's will, remember that man is not perfect, and we all make mistakes. Most times adultery is a combination of the actions of both parties. Remember God protects us from the wiles of the devil but sometimes freewill can allow us to be our own worst enemies.

This adulterous situation is a direct result of the imperfectness of man, wrong choices that were made, and the input of the devil as well. No matter the cause, you must realize and know in your heart that God did not do this to you for any reason. He is not in any way sitting on His throne pulling strings and you are not a puppet being controlled. Imperfect people living in an imperfect world full of evil can and will cause you to endure pain, strife, hardships, and detours on this journey of life.

God loves you and does not want any hurt or harm to come to you. He wants the best for you and has that planned for you. So, NO, it is not His fault. He did not do this to you to punish you. God is there to comfort you and guide through and out of this darkness. Trust Him. Do not blame Him.

Scriptures

"When God created mankind, he made them in the likeness of God. He created them male and female and blessed them. And he named them "Mankind" when they were created". ~ **Genesis 5:1**

"Dear friends, let us love one another, for love comes from God. Everyone who loves has been born of God and knows God. Whoever does not love does not know God, because God is love. This is how God showed His love among us: He sent His one and only Son into the world that we might live through Him. This is love: not that we loved God, but that he loved us and sent His Son as an atoning sacrifice for our sins". ~ **1 John 4:7-10**

"This only have I found: God created mankind upright, but they have gone in search of many schemes". ~ **Ecclesiastes 7:29**

Be alert and of sober mind. Your enemy the devil prowls around like a roaring lion looking for someone to devour. Resist Him, standing firm in the faith, because you know that the family of believers throughout the world is undergoing the same kind of sufferings". ~ **1 Peter 5:8-9**

Prayer

Dear God,

Please forgive me for even thinking that You could want me to suffer. You sent your perfect Son, Jesus Christ, to die for me out of love. You created me out of love. You love me and your desire is for me to do well and be blessed. I trust You God. Please help me to totally trust in You to get me through this time of pain and hurt. Forgive me for all my wrong choices and help me heal. I love and need You God, now and always. Thank You for loving me and guiding me through my past, present, and future. I know You are there and love me.

In Jesus' Name, I pray!
Amen!

Scriptures

"Remind the people to be subject to rulers and authorities, to be obedient, to be ready to do whatever is good, to slander no one, to be peaceable and considerate, and always to be gentle toward everyone". ~ **Titus 3:1-2**

"Our people must learn to devote themselves to doing what is good, in order to provide for urgent needs and not live unproductive lives". ~ **Titus 3:14**

"For God is not a God of disorder but of peace—as in all the congregations of the Lord's people". ~ **1 Corinthians 14:33**

"But I tell you, love your enemies and pray for those who persecute you", ~ **Matthew 5:44**

Gina Erwin

Prayer

Dear Father in Heaven,

I feel something is wrong in my relationship. I need to know what is going on and what I should do. God please reveal what I need to know and give me the strength to deal with it. Give me the wisdom to remain calm and react in a manner proper to your will.
God if nothing is wrong, then make it clear and show me the reason. I am feeling this way. With You God I can get through anything. Stay with me and hold me close. Allow me to know all I need to.
Thank You for a spirit of discernment and for strengthening me as I go forward doing my best to please You.

In Jesus' Name
Amen

Putting the Pieces Back Together After Divorce

Date: _____

_____

_____
_____
_____
_____
_____
_____
_____
_____
_____
_____

Day Seven

Misconception #2: It is her fault. She went after my husband.

The next area of blame tends to go towards the other woman. She was aware he was married. She wanted your man. She did everything in her power and she finally got Him. These thoughts go through your head. You call her everything, but a child of God and your anger is great towards her. However, this is also a misconception and a wrong judgement.

Even if she did set out to get your mate, it is still not her fault. Okay, now you are thinking I am crazy for even penning something like that. However, it is the truth. Whether the other woman knew of you, was an acquaintance of yours, or was your best friend, it is not her fault. She was wrong if she knew he was married, and she will answer to God for her wrongdoing. The only way it was her fault is if she held a gun to your mate's head and forced Him to have relations with her. If she did that, it is rape, not adultery, and the police need to be called. If this is the case, your mate did not commit adultery, he was violated. You need to love and care for Him.

On the other hand, if your mate did commit adultery, the other woman had no obligations to you. She did not commit to or make vows with you. She was not in a relationship with you and owed you nothing. She is not the one who broke her vows.

Blaming, striking out, screaming at, or trying to hurt her is wrong. Vengeance belongs to God and she will stand before God on judgement day.

It is not the other woman's fault and she owes you nothing. It would be great if women did not find it so easy to sleep with married men. However, it is an indicator and effect of the imperfect people we are and the imperfect world we live in. So please, as much as you may want to disburse mistreatment on her for the betrayal perpetrated against you, do not. She is not the one who hurt you and caused you pain. Your mate is the one responsible for this. Even punishing Him is wrong because as I said earlier, vengeance belongs to God alone. You should be focusing on yourself and getting through this situation. You have many decisions to make and need a clear mind to make the right ones.

Scriptures

"Do not judge, and you will not be judged. Do not condemn, and you will not be condemned. Forgive, and you will be forgiven. Give, and it will be given to you. A good measure, pressed down, shaken together, and running over, will be poured into your lap. For with the measure you use, it will be measured to you". ~ **Luke 6:37-38**

"But you, Lord Almighty, who judge righteously and test the heart and mind, let me see your vengeance on them, for to you I have committed my cause". ~ **Jeremiah 11:20**

"Do not repay anyone evil for evil. Be careful to do what is right in the eyes of everyone. If it is possible, as far as it depends on you, live at peace with everyone. Do not take revenge, my dear friends, but leave room for God's wrath, for it is written: "It is mine to avenge; I will repay", says the Lord. On the contrary: "If your enemy is hungry, feed Him; if he is thirsty, give Him something to drink. In doing this, you will heap burning coals on His head". Do not be overcome by evil, but overcome evil with good". ~ **Romans 12:17-21**

Prayer

Dear Father in Heaven,

I am upset right now, and it seems with the wrong person. While that woman had relations with my husband, she had no obligations to me. Please help me to see and know this completely. Please help me to focus on healing and lead me to the correct decisions that I need to make to move on from this situation. God draw me close to You. Please quiet my anger towards her and let me allow You to deal with her. I have no right to judge her as I do not want to be judged. Forgive any wrong actions I may have taken and guide me back to the path You have set for me. I love and need You God! I need You now. I need your love, grace, mercy, and forgiveness. Please hold on to me and allow me to see the light at the end of the tunnel. Thank You, God for all You are doing to help, guide, and protect me.

In Jesus' Name, I Pray
Amen!

Gina Erwin

My Journal

Date: _____

Day Eight

Misconception #3: My mate did this on purpose. He wanted to hurt me.

It is so easy to want to blame someone. Now that you are not blaming God or the other woman, why not blame your mate. He is the one who performed outside of His vows to you. Is it not His fault?

Some men have a sexual addiction known as nymphomania. These men are addicted to having sex constantly and often is not looking for intimacy. Nymphomaniacs would rather be single than commit to one woman because one woman usually cannot satisfy His ongoing insatiability. Having sex for a nymphomaniac is nourishing His addiction.

Nine times out of ten, the average person does not set out to commit adultery. He may be lacking and in need of a feature that he is not getting at home. Again, please know that I am in no fashion saying it is your fault. In our fast-paced imperfect world, people are progressing daily, trying to work, maintain home, supervise the kids, and preserve a wholesome marriage. Details and matters become forgotten or are overlooked which can lead to individuals feeling unloved or in a state of lack. Most times individuals do not even realize they were lacking or in need of anything until they are obtaining it from somewhere outside their relationship and are feeling content suddenly. Events happen and we all make mistakes. He may have obtained the one item he needed purely accidentally and before he could stop Himself was in a bad and wrong situation. More than likely, he never stopped long enough to even imagine the pain and repercussions that would be emitted from His actions.

Occasionally, there are men who just want to have sex with women and experience euphoria by being a type of Casanova. Rarely do these men commit and get married.

Whatever the case, I seriously doubt that your mate decided to commit adultery just to hurt you. Our flesh is weak, and it is easy for imperfect people to make mistakes that cause tremendous pain on others. Errors are going to happen. How you deal with them is the greatest factor. You must deal with them in a God pleasing manner for it to work out for your good.

I am going to put myself out there and be totally transparent. I committed adultery in my first marriage. Please believe me when I say, it just happened. I was spending time with someone due to my occupation and we just clicked. Before I realized it, I was getting the attention and affection I did not even realize I desired. I let it go too far. My husband never found out. However, we did divorce years later. I am saying this, so you know that although you have experienced a great deal of pain, it is unlikely your husband set out to intentionally cause it. Yes, he did, and he must answer for it. However, the punishment and judgement are not yours to hand out. It is God's.

My second husband committed adultery on me, and it hurt like Hades. I guess I could say you reap what you sew. That may be the case and it may not. No matter what the case is, we all must look to God to get through and get back on the right path. This means dealing with the situation and allowing God to oversee judgement and punishment.

Scriptures

"For all have sinned and fall short of the glory of God", ~ **Romans 3:23**
"You have heard that it was said, 'Love your neighbor and hate your enemy'. But I tell you, love your enemies and pray for those who persecute you", ~ **Matthew 5:43-44**

"Do not judge, or you too will be judged. For in the same way you judge others, you will be judged, and with the measure you use, it will be measured to you". ~ **Matthew 7:1-2**

"Do not be deceived: God cannot be mocked. A man reaps what he sows. Whoever sows to please their flesh, from the flesh will reap destruction; whoever sows to please the Spirit, from the Spirit will reap eternal life. Let us not become weary in doing good, for at the proper time we will reap a harvest if we do not give up. Therefore, as we have opportunity, let us do good to all people, especially to those who belong to the family of believers".
~ **Galatians 6:7-10**

Gina Erwin

Prayer

Dear Lord,

I have been hurt by the man I love. It is so painful, and I do not understand why he has chosen to do this unthinkable thing. I want to assess blame, but it is not my call, it is yours. Help me to deal with this situation and my mate in a manner that is pleasing to You. Guide and lead me God. Quiet my anger and desire for revenge. Help me rely on You. Humble me and give me a spirit of forgiveness and the knowledge to do the right thing from this point forward. God thank You for your wisdom, grace, mercy, and love.

In Jesus' Name, I Pray
Amen!

Putting the Pieces Back Together After Divorce

Date: _____

_____
_____
_____
_____
_____
_____
_____
_____
_____
_____
_____
_____
_____
_____

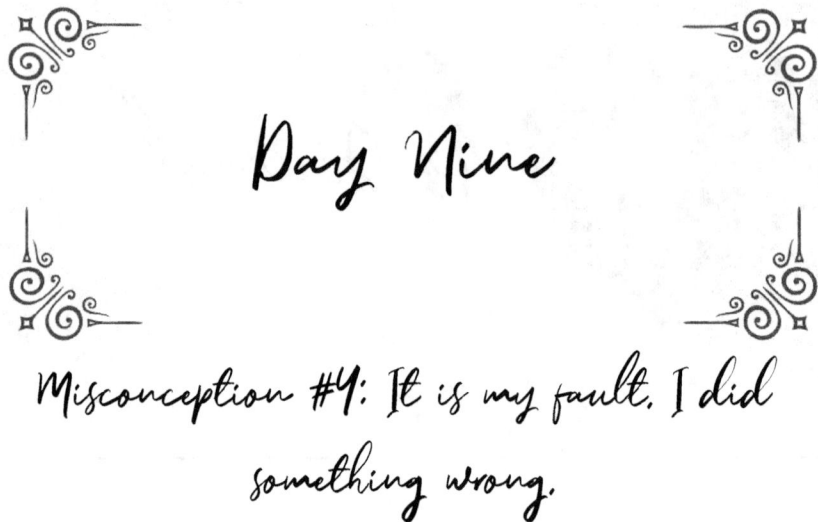

Day Nine

Misconception #4: It is my fault. I did something wrong.

Self-blaming is also a reaction of adultery. You may think that you were not attentive enough to His needs or that you did not do what you were supposed as a wife.

A marriage is a collaboration of a husband and a wife with the guidance of God. It is a three-fold bond that requires communication, trust, and dedication. Daily communication with God and each other, trusting God and each other, and being dedicated to God and each other is necessary for a marriage to succeed. Both parties must do their part. Some say it is a 50 ~ 50 relationship. I disagree. It is a 100 ~ 100 relationship. Both parties must give their all for a marriage to work. The problem comes in when God is left out of the equation. Without God in the marriage, the repercussions of the state of humanity makes it easier for someone to do the wrong thing.

No one is perfect and we all make mistakes. Sometimes those mistakes are devastating and hard to come back from. In this case, adultery, can end marriages and cause severe devastation.

Blaming yourself is wrong. While you may have made some mistakes, you did not make Him commit adultery. You did not deserve this pain and betrayal. It is not your fault.

Scriptures

"Submit to one another out of reverence for Christ. Wives submit yourselves to your own husbands as you do to the Lord. For the husband is the head of the wife as Christ is the head of the church, His body, of which he is the Savior. Now as the church submits to Christ, so also wives should submit to their husbands in everything. Husbands, love your wives, just as Christ loved the church and gave Himself up for her to make her holy, cleansing her by the washing with water through the word, and to present her to Himself as a radiant church, without stain or wrinkle or any other blemish, but holy and blameless. In this same way, husbands ought to love their wives as their own bodies. He who loves His wife loves Himself. After all, no one ever hated their own body, but they feed and care for their body, just as Christ does the church— for we are members of His body. "For this reason, a man will leave His father and mother and be united to His wife, and the two will become one flesh". This is a profound mystery—but I am talking about Christ and the church. However, each one of you also must love His wife as he loves Himself, and the wife must respect her husband". ~ **Ephesian 5:21-33**

"Haven't you read," he replied, "that at the beginning the Creator 'made them male and female, and said, 'For this reason a man will leave His father and mother and be united to His wife, and the two will become one flesh? So, they are no longer two, but one flesh. Therefore, what God has joined together, let no one separate". ~ **Matthew 19:4-6**

"For all have sinned and fall short of the glory of God", ~ **Romans 3:23**

Gina Erwin

Prayer

Dear God,

Help me. I know I am not perfect, and neither is my husband. He has committed adultery and I do not understand why. I want to blame someone, and I am wondering if this is my fault. I need your wisdom and knowledge to know what to do and why this has happened to me. No one is better than anyone else and neither am I. If I did anything wrong God, please forgive me. Console me and guide me going forward to not issue blame to anyone including myself. You are the ONE that everyone must answer to, not me. Help me to remain faithful to You and have faith in You. Only You can fix this and repair me. Thank You for loving me.

In Jesus' Name
Amen

Putting the Pieces Back Together After Divorce

Date: _____

_____
_____
_____
_____
_____
_____
_____
_____
_____
_____
_____
_____
_____
_____

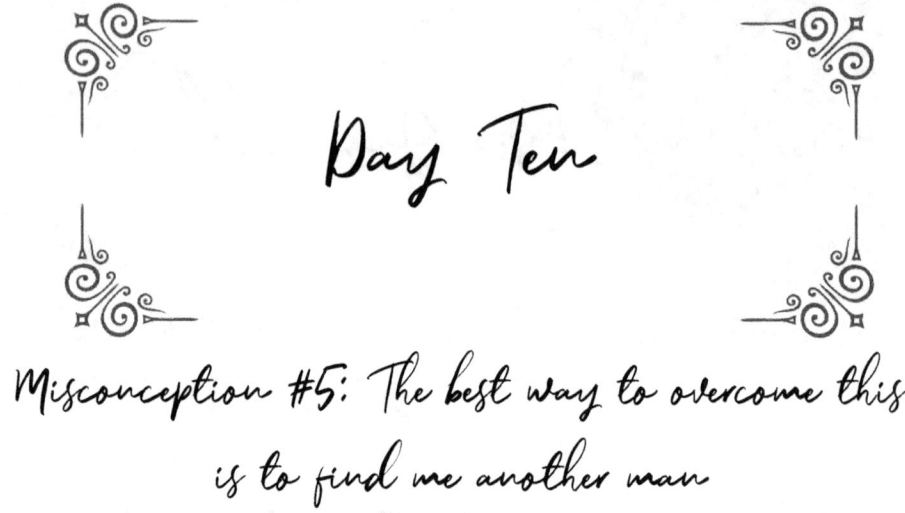

Day Ten

Misconception #5: The best way to overcome this is to find me another man

We all have those true loving friends that will tell us not to let it get us down and just find someone else. "You deserve someone who will treat you like the queen you are!" You may even think about getting back at your mate by doing the same thing to Him, so he knows how it feels. These concepts sound good at this moment but they are wrong. You do deserve to be loved and treated like a queen, but now is not the time.

Adding another person to the current problematic situation is not the answer. There is already three people and two households not counting any children involved. It would not be smart to involve someone else in this at the current time. You are blameless right now. Forming a relationship with another man before you are divorced would make you guilty of adultery also.

Any relationship formed in the middle of this contemptuous situation will not only fail but will exasperate the situation to a greater level of craziness. All you can offer right now is pain and confusion. While gaining the attention of another man might make you forget for a moment, it will not make the situation go away. It will only complicate it and make it more complex. Two wrongs do not make a right.

Now is the time for looking to God, acknowledging, discerning, comprehending, forgiving, decision-making, healing and moving forward. Each of these elements are a process within themselves and will take time to venture through. Complete healing incorporates these and more before you can move forward and offer yourself to someone else completely.

Acting on impulse and out of emotion is easy to do in your current position. However, acting in wisdom will lead you to a position of positivity, self-love, and becoming a virtuous woman of God. In turn, you will be blameless and ready for the man God has prepared for you.

I jumped into a new relationship before my first marriage was over and it did not end well. I placed Him before God and threw myself into Him and the love he offered me. It ended in adultery and extensive overwhelming pain and hurt. So, please fix yourself and love yourself before inviting someone else into your life. We all desire to be loved because we are created in love to be loved.

So, finding a new man is not the answer. You need to find yourself first and deal with everything before moving onto the next relationship. Some of us do not think we like being alone. However, you are not alone. God is always with you and He will guide you through.

Scriptures

"You shall not commit adultery!" ~ **Exodus 20:14**

"But a man who commits adultery has no sense; whoever does so, destroys Himself". ~ **Proverbs 6:32**

"The blameless spend their days under the Lord's care, and their inheritance will endure forever. In times of disaster they will not wither; in days of famine they will enjoy plenty". ~ **Psalms 37:1819**

"A wife of noble character who can find? She is worth far more than rubies. Her husband has full confidence in her and lacks nothing of value. She brings Him good, not harm, all the days of her life. She selects wool and flax and works with eager hands. She is like the merchant ships, bringing her food from afar. She gets up while it is still night; she provides food for her family and portions for her female servants. She considers a field and buys it; out of her earnings she plants a vineyard. She sets about her work vigorously; her arms are strong for her tasks. She sees that her trading is profitable, and her lamp does not go out at night. In her hand, she holds the distaff and grasps the spindle with her fingers. She opens her arms to the poor and extends her hands to the needy. When it snows, she has no fear for her household; for all of them are clothed in scarlet. She makes coverings for her bed; she is clothed in fine linen and purple. Her husband is respected at the city gate, where he takes His seat among the elders of the land. She makes linen garments and sells them and supplies the merchants with sashes. She is clothed with strength and dignity; she can laugh at the days to come. She speaks with wisdom, and faithful instruction is on her tongue. She watches over the affairs of her household and does not eat the bread of idleness. Her children arise and call her blessed; her husband also, and he praises her: "Many women do noble things, but you surpass them all". Charm is

deceptive, and beauty is fleeting; but a woman who fears the Lord is to be praised. Honor her for all that her hands have done, and let her works bring her praise at the city gate". ~
Proverbs 31:10-31

Gina Erwin

Prayer

Dear God,

I am in pain. My heart is hurting. My husband, **(say husband's name),** has committed adultery against me and I am not sure what to do. My flesh wants revenge. Yet my spirit is crying out to You for guidance. Please help me act out of wisdom and your principles, not out of my pain and anger. God help me to feel your presence and know that I am not alone. You are with me. Ease my pain and guide me forward Lord. Let me make the right decisions to remain blameless in this situation and become a stronger virtuous woman after all is settled. Thank You, God for loving me, healing me, and guiding me forward.

In Jesus' Name,
Amen!

Putting the Pieces Back Together After Divorce

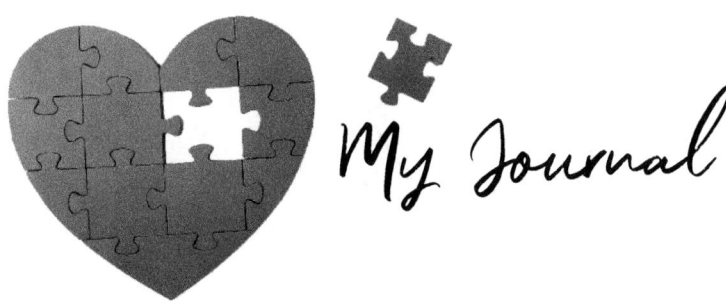

Date: _____

_____
_____
_____
_____
_____
_____
_____
_____
_____
_____
_____
_____

Day Eleven

Misconception #6: I will be fine. This will not affect me.

One of the worst things you can do is underestimate the gravity of the situation. This situation has hit you right in the core of your being, your heart. Yes, eventually, you will be fine. However, this situation is going to affect you, your future decisions, your outlook, and how you approach your future. These affects do not by any means need to be negative. By going through the process calmly in wisdom, being patient, relying on God, and addressing all areas of adultery and your situation, you will be fine. Yes, you will have scars and memories, however you will attain the ability to live a prosperous and successful life.

    You need to deal with this situation physically, emotionally, mentally, and spiritually. Physically, you can feel like you have been beat down. Emotionally, there is a full spectrum of different emotions that you will go through, such as sorrow, anger, pity, and many more that we will address later in the book. Mentally, you will feel drained and even desire to give up. Give in, but never give up. Spiritually, you can feel lost, absent of God, confused as to what the purpose of this situation is.

    Right here and now, realize adultery has occurred and you have been affected by it. Not only have you already been affected, you will be affected for an added time. You have a process to go through and until you do, adultery is going to affect you.

The big question here is, how will you allow it to affect you? Will you use it as a learning experience? Will you let it defeat you or take you to the next level? Will this just be a test, or will you exit with a testimony that will help other women in your situation? The answers are your free choice. You can let it make you or break you.

In my wildest dreams, I had no idea that my personal experience with adultery would lead to authoring this book, but it did. God moved my heart to help others going through the same type pain and torment I endured due to adultery. If this book brings glory to God and helps just one person hurting from adultery, I have accomplished my goal.

My prayer is that right now you have decided that this situation will make you wiser and capable of what God has planned for you. You can learn and go forward to help other women going through the things you have experienced. Your testimony will glorify God and help others to know Him. If you are obedient and draw close to God, He will use this situation for your good and remove the remnants of pain.

Scriptures

"But how is it to your credit if you receive a beating for doing wrong and endure it? But if you suffer for doing good and you endure it, this is commendable before God". ~ **1 Peter 2:20**

"His divine power has given us everything we need for a Godly life through our knowledge of Him who called us by His own glory and goodness. Through these he has given us His very great and precious promises, so that through them you may participate in the divine nature, having escaped the corruption in the world caused by evil desires. For this very reason, make every effort to add to your faith goodness; and to goodness, knowledge; and to knowledge, self-control; and to self-control, perseverance; and to perseverance, Godliness; and to Godliness, mutual affection; and to mutual affection, love. For if you possess these qualities in increasing measure, they will keep you from being ineffective and unproductive in your knowledge of our Lord Jesus Christ. But whoever does not have them is nearsighted and blind, forgetting that they have been cleansed from their past sins". ~ **2 Peter 1:39**

"I consider that our present sufferings are not worth comparing with the glory that will be revealed in us. For the creation waits in eager expectation for the children of God to be revealed. For the creation was subjected to frustration, not by its own choice, but by the will of the one who subjected it, in hope that the creation itself will be liberated from its bondage to decay and brought into the freedom and glory of the children of God. We know that the whole creation has been groaning as in the pains of childbirth right up to the present time. Not only so, but we ourselves, who have the first fruits of the Spirit, groan inwardly as we wait eagerly for our adoption to sonship, the redemption of our bodies. For in this hope we were saved. But hope that is seen is no hope at all. Who hopes for what they already have? But if we hope for what we do not yet have, we wait for it patiently. In the same way, the Spirit helps us in our weakness. We do not know what we ought to pray for, but the Spirit Himself intercedes for us through wordless groans. And he who searches our hearts knows the mind of the Spirit, because the Spirit intercedes for God's people in accordance with the will of God. And we know that in all things God works for the good of those who love Him, who have been called according to His purpose". ~ **Romans 8:18-28**

"For this reason, I remind you to fan into flame the gift of God, which is in you through the laying on of my hands. For the Spirit God gave us does not make us timid, but gives us power, love, and self-discipline. So, do not be ashamed of the testimony about our Lord or of me His prisoner. Rather, join with me in suffering for the gospel, by the power of God. He has saved us and called us to a holy life—not because of anything we have done but because of His own purpose and grace. This grace was given us in Christ Jesus before the beginning of time, but it has now been revealed through the appearing of our Savior, Christ Jesus, who has destroyed death and has brought life and immortality to light through the gospel. And of this gospel I was appointed a herald and an apostle and a teacher. That is why I am suffering as I am. Yet this is no cause for shame, because I know whom I have believed, and am convinced that he is able to guard what I have entrusted to Him until that day". ~ **2 Timothy 1:6-12**

Gina Erwin

Prayer

Father in Heaven,

I do not understand all of what I am experiencing. I am confused. Help me to see and hear You. Help my faith grow and sustain me during this test. Allow me to use this experience to learn, help others, and glorify your name. With You, I will not just survive, I will grow spiritually, gain a greater relationship with You, attain new abilities, and be the daughter You want me to be. Thank You, God for all You do and will do. Thank You for getting me through this and all things. I love and need You God!

In Jesus' Name,
Amen!

Putting the Pieces Back Together After Divorce

Date: _____

_____
_____
_____
_____
_____
_____
_____
_____
_____
_____
_____
_____
_____

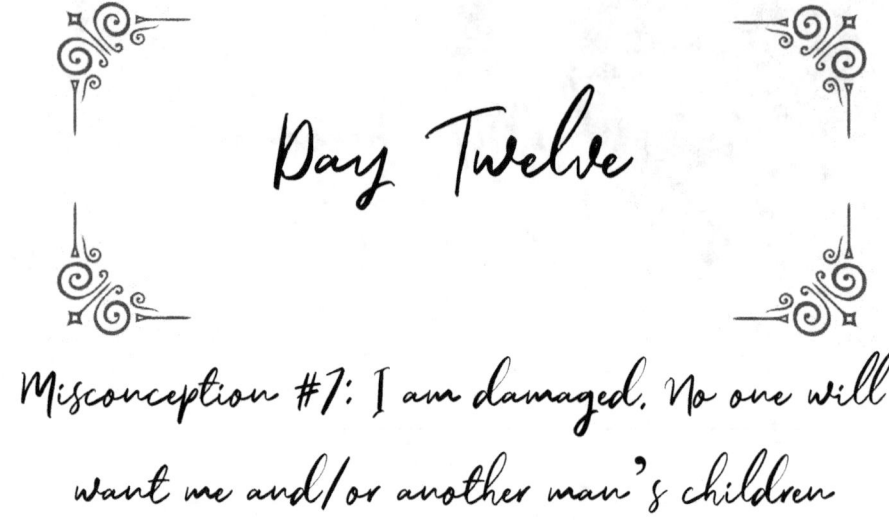

Day Twelve

Misconception #7: I am damaged. No one will want me and/or another man's children

I am not good enough. I have been hurt. No man will want me. All these thoughts come into your head and may have even be said by your spouse to defer blame. This is in no way true.

You are a daughter of the KING. God created you and He does not make mistakes. While we are imperfect, we are still good enough to receive God's love and if we are not good enough for any imperfect man, then that man does not deserve us to begin with. Even if you have children, a real man will respect their relationship with their biological father (if one exists) and love those children because he loves you and they are a part of you.

We are all imperfect and have been damaged (hurt) by the experiences of our life. What we must do is forgive those who hurt us and move on. No one is exempt from pain and hurt. Remember Jesus was mocked, beat, and crucified for our sins. He was guilty of nothing. We who fall short of pleasing God daily, should not expect to be shielded from it. Just as Jesus did, we must take the hurt, pain, and damage and use it to proclaim God's love and glory.

God loves you and He will send the right man to you when the time is right. God's time does not always mean now in our time. When the time is right it will happen. Until then, concentrate on your personal relationship with God and walk in your purpose.

God loves you as you are, as He created you. The man God has for you will too.

Scriptures

"What, then, shall we say in response to these things? If God is for us, who can be against us? He who did not spare His own Son, but gave Him up for us all—how will he not also, along with Him, graciously give us all things? Who will bring any charge against those whom God has chosen? It is God who justifies. Who then is the one who condemns? No one. Christ Jesus who died—more than that, who was raised to life—is at the right hand of God and is also interceding for us. Who shall separate us from the love of Christ? Shall trouble or hardship or persecution or famine or nakedness or danger or sword? As it is written: "For your sake we face death all day long; we are considered as sheep to be slaughtered". No, in all these things we are more than conquerors through Him who loved us. For I am convinced that neither death nor life, neither angels nor demons, neither the present nor the future, nor any powers, neither height nor depth, nor anything else in all creation, will be able to separate us from the love of God that is in Christ Jesus our Lord." ~ **Romans 8:31-39**

"Your beauty should not come from outward adornment, such as elaborate hairstyles and the wearing of gold jewelry or fine clothes. Rather, it should be that of your inner self, the unfading beauty of a gentle and quiet spirit, which is of great worth in
God's sight". ~ **1 Peter 3:3-4**

"For you created my inmost being; you knit me together in my mother's womb. I praise you because I am fearfully and wonderfully made; your works are wonderful; I know that full well. My frame was not hidden from you when I was made in the secret place, when I was woven together in the depths of the earth. Your eyes saw my unformed body; all the days ordained for me were written in your book before one of them came to be. How precious to me are your thoughts, God! How vast is the sum of them! Were I to count them, they would outnumber the grains of sand - when I awake, I am still with you". ~ **Psalms 139:13-18**

"But do not forget this one thing, dear friends: With the Lord a day is like a thousand years, and a thousand years are like a day. The Lord is not slow in keeping His promise, as some understand slowness. Instead he is patient with you, not wanting anyone to perish, but everyone to come to repentance". ~ **2 Peter 3:8-9**

Gina Erwin

Prayer

Dearest God,

Thank You for creating me. Help me to see what You see in me and the purpose You created me for. Help me know that I am worthy of love and that in the right time You will send the man for me. Give me patience God. Reveal Your purpose for me and help me stay on the right path to fulfilling it. God, You are all I need but I do desire companionship. If it is your will send Him to me in your time frame and not mine. It is your will that must be done. Thank You for your mercy, forgiveness, and love.

In Jesus' Name,
Amen

Putting the Pieces Back Together After Divorce

Date: _____

_____
_____
_____
_____
_____
_____
_____
_____
_____
_____
_____
_____
_____

Day Thirteen

Misconception #8: I cannot go on

Adultery causes pain. You will hurt mental and physically from adultery. Why does it hurt so much? It is because you have suffered a break and a loss. Sacred vows between you and your spouse, expectations, and your trust have been broken. If separation and divorce are a result, you have in fact lost your spouse and just like losing someone to death it hurts and causes pain.

It is okay to hurt and feel like you want to give in. What you cannot do is give up and remain in the hurt and pain. No one except God should have the power to make you want to give up and end your life. God would never do that to you because you are special to Him. He loves you and created you for a purpose.

*** If you are contemplating suicide or are in a place where you have totally given up, I need you to STOP and call one or all the following:

- 💜 God (prayer)
- 💜 Your Pastor or a Pastor/Minister you know and trust
- 💜 (800) 273-8255 The National Suicide Prevention Lifeline
- 💜 A friend and/or family member

Be truthful with them about what you are feeling and contemplating. Listen to them and trust God to show you the way back from the edge.

Putting the Pieces Back Together After Divorce

You are special to God and have a purpose. It is time to seek out God and your purpose. Use the pain to power your purpose and move forward. There is a reason for this pain and a time for everything. There is a time to live and a time to die, but the choice is God's, not yours.

When I encountered adultery, I was there, and I wanted to give up. I did not want to feel that pain anymore. What stopped me was my God and my youngest daughter. I knew God loved me and I had a purpose to fulfill for Him. I felt that my two oldest children could go on without me. They were grown and had families of their own. However, I knew my teenager needed me to be there for her and I did not want her to believe that I did not love her enough to stay here. I want her to be a strong woman when she grows up and this would not be an example of that to her. In this instance I realized why the miracle of my daughter's existence occurred, for a time such as this. I also had a Godly friend who spoke life into me, listened to me cry, allowed me to vent, shared her experiences, and prayed over me constantly for weeks. Some days she would pray for me two or more times daily. The number did not matter, she prayed as much as I needed her to. Some nights her prayers were the only reason I slept. God placed her in my life for this purpose and I will love and cherish her forever.

Today I am moving forward in the power of God and in the love of my family and friends. I have taken that pain and used it in beginning to fulfill the purpose God has for me. The test adultery presented to me is now my testimony. The pain powers my purpose. I want to use the experience to empower you and other women to trust God, keep pushing forward, and help others. **Do not let anything or anyone make you feel worthless. You are a child of God, loved, special, and have a purpose.**

Scriptures

"For you created my inmost being; you knit me together in my mother's womb. I praise you because I am fearfully and wonderfully made; your works are wonderful; I know that full well". ~ **Psalms 139: 13-14**

"There is a time for everything, and a season for every activity under the heavens: a time to be born and a time to die, a time to plant and a time to uproot, a time to kill and a time to heal, a time to tear down and a time to build, a time to weep and a time to laugh, a time to mourn and a time to dance, a time to scatter stones and a time to gather them, a time to embrace and a time to refrain from embracing, a time to search and a time to give up, a time to keep and a time to throw away, a time to tear and a time to mend, a time to be silent and a time to speak, a time to love and a time to hate, a time for war and a time for peace." ~ **Ecclesiastes 3:1-8**

"But you are a chosen people, a royal priesthood, a holy nation, God's special possession, that you may declare the praises of Him who called you out of darkness into His wonderful light. Once you were not a people, but now you are the people of God; once you had not received mercy, but now you have received mercy". ~ **1 Peter 2:9-10**

For it is commendable if someone bears up under the pain of unjust suffering because they are conscious of God. But how is it to your credit if you receive a beating for doing wrong and endure it? But if you suffer for doing good and you endure it, this is commendable before God. To this you were called, because Christ suffered for you, leaving you an example, that you should follow in His steps". ~ **1 Peter 2:19-21**

"I lift up my eyes to the mountains - where does my help come from? My help comes from the Lord, the Maker of heaven and earth. He will not let your foot slip - he who watches over you will not slumber; indeed, he who watches over Israel will neither slumber nor sleep. The Lord watches over you - the Lord is your shade at your right hand; the sun will not harm you by day, nor the moon by night. The Lord will keep you from all harm - he will watch over your life; the Lord will watch over your coming and going both now and forevermore". ~ **Psalm 121: 1-8**

"Is anyone among you in trouble? Let them pray. Is anyone happy? Let them sing songs of praise. Is anyone among you sick? Let them call the elders of the church to pray over them and anoint them with oil in the name of the Lord. And the prayer offered in faith will make the sick person well; the Lord will raise them up. If they have sinned, they will be forgiven. Therefore, confess your sins to each other and pray for each other so that you may be healed. The prayer of a righteous person is powerful and effective". ~ **James 5:13-16**

"I call on you, my God, for you will answer me; turn your ear to me and hear my prayer. Show me the wonders of your great love, you who save by your right hand those who take refuge in you from their foes. Keep me as the apple of your eye; hide me in the shadow of your wings from the wicked who are out to destroy me, from my mortal enemies who surround me". ~ **Psalm 17: 69**

"Jesus looked at them and said, "With man this is impossible, but with God all things are possible". ~ **Matthew 19:26**

Gina Erwin

Prayer

Dear God,

I come to You in pain feeling **(state your feelings)**. I want to give up. It hurts so bad. I know that I am your child and special in your sight. Help me see what You see in me. Give me the desire to move forward, putting You and my purpose first. God, please do not allow this deceit to hurt me beyond repair. Ease my pain and show me how to use it to bring You glory and praise while fulfilling the purpose you have assigned me. Place people around me that will help me focus on You, pray for me, pray with me, and help me walk in my purpose. God, remove those who will see me hurt and persecute me. Pick me up and place my feet back on solid ground. Please strengthen me and apply wisdom, knowledge, and understanding in my life. Thank You, God, for creating and loving me. I love You and in You I can go on and do anything I set my mind to if it is in accordance with your will.

In Jesus, Name,
Amen

Putting the Pieces Back Together After Divorce

My Journal

Date: _____

83

Day Fourteen

Acknowledgement

Now that we have dealt with the misconceptions and wrong components of adultery, it is time to move forward and stand as a child of God through the process. Your first step is acknowledgement. You must realize and acknowledge that this situation has occurred, and you must deal with it.

This may be hard to do, but it is just the beginning of the process. If you must, use a mirror as you state the facts. Tell yourself that the man you love has committed adultery and hurt you to your core. Tell yourself you are beautiful and did not deserve this pain, betrayal, and hurt. Look deep and try to see what God sees in you. Finally tell yourself that this too shall pass, and that God has your back and will guide you through all the difficulties.

Scriptures

"For you created my inmost being; you knit me together in my mother's womb. I praise you because I am fearfully and wonderfully made; your works are wonderful; I know that full well". ~ **Psalms 139: 13-14**

"To the Jews who had believed Him, Jesus said, "If you hold to my teaching, you are really my disciples. Then you will know the truth, and the truth will set you free". ~ **John 8:31-32**

"For I am convinced that neither death nor life, neither angels nor demons, neither the present nor the future, nor any powers, neither height nor depth, nor anything else in all creation, will be able to separate us from the love of God that is in Christ Jesus our Lord." ~ **Romans 8:38-39**

Gina Erwin

Prayer

Dear Father in Heaven,

I am walking in my reality. My spouse has hurt me. Help me look past the pain and see what You see in me. Let me use this experience to strengthen myself, walk in my purpose, glorify your Name, and help others. Allow me to see the beauty of my spirit and know that while this situation has occurred, it will not define me. I am your daughter and I am wonderfully made to be loved and fulfill the purpose you have chosen for me. Guide me from this point forward and keep me on the right path. Thank You, God, for your unconditional love, mercy, and grace.

In Jesus' Holy Name
Amen

Putting the Pieces Back Together After Divorce

Date: _____

_____

_____
_____
_____
_____
_____
_____
_____
_____
_____
_____

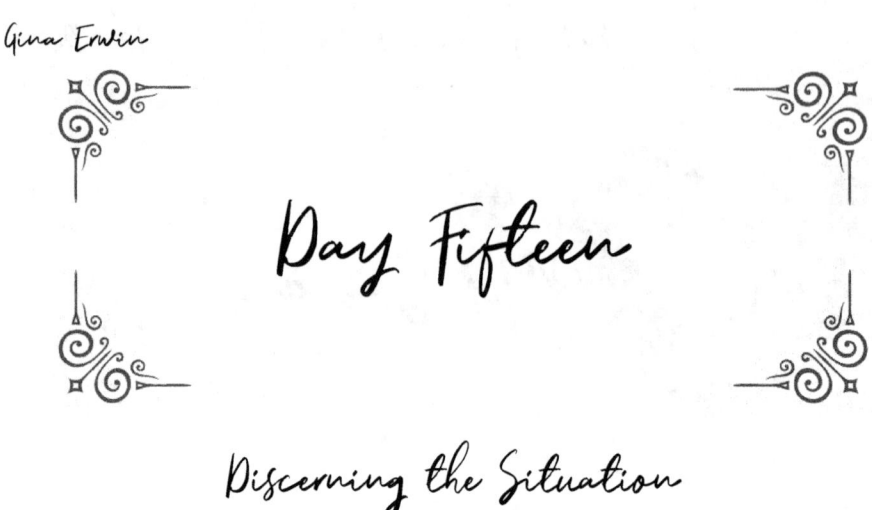

Day Fifteen

Discerning the Situation

You have acknowledged the situation. Your spouse has committed adultery. Now is the time for discernment. You need to discern all the aspects of the situation. This will be different for each woman reading this because it depends on your personal circumstances.

Discerning the situation involves understanding of the big picture. Did the adultery occur once or was it an ongoing thing? Is it still going on even after being exposed? Do you want to remain in this relationship? Does your spouse want to remain in the relationship? Are there children involved in your home or the home of the other woman? Is your spouse the father of any of her children? Do the children know? How do the children feel about it? If they do not know, how will this affect them? Is there a possibility of diseases being passed around? What is your current financial situation? If you chose to separate, how will you divide things? Where will the children's primary residence be? Can you both be cordial and get through this without ugliness occurring? Is counseling a choice? Is reconciliation a possibility? Is divorce the only way to go? What is the Godly thing to do? What does God require of me?

These are just some of the things you must look at and some of the questions that need to be answered to know the depth of the situation and what can be done moving forward. Here is where everyone's situation differs. You must discern your situation and make the proper decisions. Look at everything involved and ask the necessary questions.

Putting the Pieces Back Together After Divorce

The answers you produce are yours and your spouse's alone. Remain in truth no matter how it may hurt. The truth will set you free and guide you to choosing the right path to take.

Pray often, even if it is multiple times a day. Lean on God to help you see the things you need to see and discern. Pray for guidance, wisdom, patience, and strength. Do not act out of anger or attempt revenge. Give it to God and do what He guides you in the spirit to do.

Whether you have easy or tough decisions to make, allow God's guidance in making them. Chose to stay virtuous in your actions and God will bless your efforts. You must know everything before trying to make decisions moving forward.

Scriptures

"In you, Lord my God, I put my trust. I trust in you; do not let me be put to shame, nor let my enemies triumph over me. No one who hopes in you will ever be put to shame, but shame will come on those who are treacherous without cause. Show me your ways, Lord, teach me your paths. Guide me in your truth and teach me, for you are God my Savior, and my hope is in you all day long." ~ **Psalm 5:1-5**

"To the Jews who had believed Him, Jesus said, "If you hold to my teaching, you are really my disciples. Then you will know the truth, and the truth will set you free". ~ **John 8: 31-32**

"For gaining wisdom and instruction; for understanding words of insight; for receiving instruction in prudent behavior, doing what is right and just and fair; for giving prudence to those who are simple, knowledge and discretion to the young - let the wise listen and add to their learning, and let the discerning get guidance - for understanding proverbs and parables, the sayings and riddles of the wise." ~ **Proverbs 1: 2-6**

"Pride goes before destruction, a haughty spirit before a fall. Better to be lowly in spirit along with the oppressed than to share plunder with the proud. Whoever gives heed to instruction prospers, and blessed is the one who trusts in the Lord. The wise in heart are called discerning, and gracious words promote instruction". ~ **Proverbs 16: 18-21**

"The one who has knowledge uses words with restraint, and whoever has understanding is even-tempered. Even fools are thought wise if they keep silent, and discerning if they hold their tongues". ~ **Proverbs 17:27-28**

"The heart of the discerning acquires knowledge, for the ears of the wise seek it out". ~ **Proverbs 18:15**

"The person without the Spirit does not accept the things that come from the Spirit of God but considers them foolishness, and cannot understand them because they are discerned only through the Spirit". ~ **1 Corinthians 2:14**

"And this is my prayer: that your love may abound more and more in knowledge and depth of insight, so that you may be able to discern what is best and may be pure and blameless for the day of Christ, filled with the fruit of righteousness that comes through
Jesus Christ - to the glory and praise of God". ~ **Philippians 1:911**

"Trust in the Lord with all your heart and lean not on your own understanding; in all your ways submit to Him, and he will make your paths straight". ~ **Proverbs 3:5-6**

Gina Erwin

Prayer

Dear God,

Guide me to the truth. Allow me to take it all in and make the right decisions according to your will. Help me to have patience and understanding to be able to look at the big picture and all that can be affected by my decisions. Give me wisdom to make the right decisions and choose the right path moving forward. Strengthen my faith in You and allow me to lean on You and not my own understanding. Thank You, God for your wisdom in dealing with this situation and your love that sustains me.

In Jesus' Name,
Amen!

Putting the Pieces Back Together After Divorce

My Journal

Date: _____

_____
_____
_____
_____
_____
_____
_____
_____
_____
_____
_____

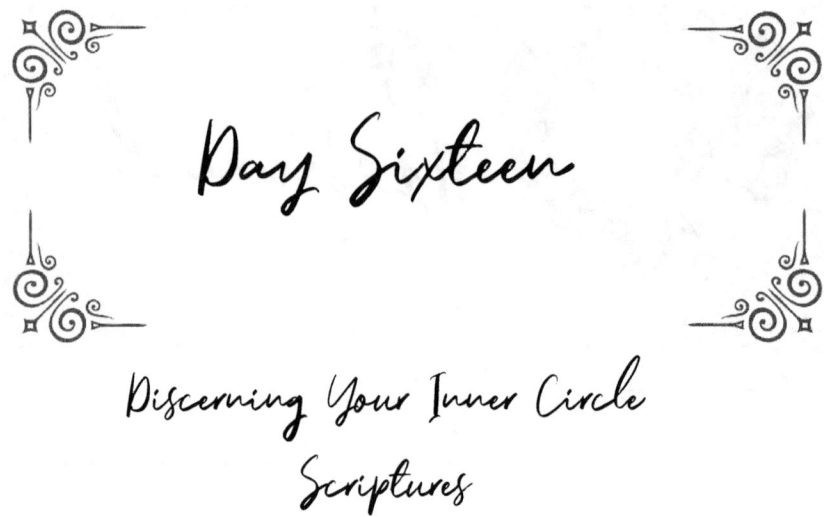

Day Sixteen

Discerning Your Inner Circle Scriptures

"Blessed are those who find wisdom, those who gain understanding, for she is more profitable than silver and yields better returns than gold. She is more precious than rubies; nothing you desire can compare with her. Long life is in her right hand; in her left hand are riches and honor. Her ways are pleasant ways, and all her paths are peace. She is a tree of life to those who take hold of her; those who hold her fast will be blessed. By wisdom, the Lord laid the earth's foundations, by understanding he set the heavens in place; by His knowledge the watery depths were divided, and the clouds let drop the dew. My son, do not let wisdom and understanding out of your sight, preserve sound judgment and discretion; they will be life for you, an ornament to grace your neck. Then you will go on your way in safety, and your foot will not stumble. When you lie down, you will not be afraid; when you lie down, your sleep will be sweet. Have no fear of sudden disaster or of the ruin that overtakes the wicked, for the Lord will be at your side and will keep your foot from being snared". ~ **Proverbs 3:13-26**

"Without wood a fire goes out; without a gossip a quarrel dies down. As charcoal to embers and as wood to fire, so is a quarrelsome person for kindling strife. The words of a gossip are like choice morsels; they go down to the inmost parts. Like a coating of silver dross on earthenware are fervent lips with an evil heart. Enemies disguise themselves with their lips, but in their hearts, they harbor deceit. Though their speech is charming, do not believe them, for seven abominations fill their hearts. Their malice may be concealed by deception, but their wickedness will be exposed in the assembly. Whoever digs a pit will fall into it; if someone rolls a stone, it will roll back on them. A lying tongue hates those it hurts, and a flattering mouth works ruin". ~ **Proverbs 26:20-28**

"Do not be misled: "Bad company corrupts good character."" ~ **1 Corinthians 15:33**

"Not a word from their mouth can be trusted; their heart is filled with malice. Their throat is an open grave; with their tongues they tell lies.: ~ **Psalm 5:9**

"I said, "I will watch my ways and keep my tongue from sin; I will put a muzzle on my mouth while in the presence of the wicked". So, I remained utterly silent, not even saying anything good. But my anguish increased; my heart grew hot within me. While I meditated, the fire burned; then I spoke with my tongue:" ~ **Psalm 39:1-3**

"The mouths of the righteous utter wisdom, and their tongues speak what is just". ~ **Psalm 37:30**

"A gossip betrays a confidence; so, avoid anyone who talks too much". ~ **Proverbs 20:9**

"Jesus, knowing all that was going to happen to Him, went out and asked them, "Who is it you want?" "Jesus of Nazareth", they replied. "I am he", Jesus said. (And Judas the traitor was standing there with them.) When Jesus said, "I am he", they drew back and fell to the ground. Again, he asked them, "Who is it you want?" "Jesus of Nazareth", they said.

Jesus answered, "I told you that I am he. If you are looking for me, then let these men go". This happened so that the words he had spoken would be fulfilled: "I have not lost one of those you gave me". Then Simon Peter, who had a sword, drew it, and struck the high priest's servant, cutting off His right ear. (The servant's name was Malchus) Jesus commanded Peter, "Put your sword away! Shall I not drink the cup the Father has given me?" ~ **John 18:1-11**

Putting the Pieces Back Together After Divorce

Prayer

Father in Heaven,

Please help me to discern my family and friends. Please remove anyone that is out to hurt or harm me. Please guide me in your wisdom when deciding who to keep close to me in this time of despair. Help those who love me not to act out of anger for my pain. Help them to advance my relationship with You. Guide them to pray with and for me instead of acting out on my behalf. Guide their tongues as well as mine. Help each of us to honor You instead of feeding into the ugliness of the current situation. Thank You, God for my inner circle and support system. Thank You for loving me when I am hurting so bad.

In Jesus' Name
Amen

Gina Erwin

Date: _____

_____
_____
_____
_____
_____
_____
_____
_____
_____
_____
_____

98

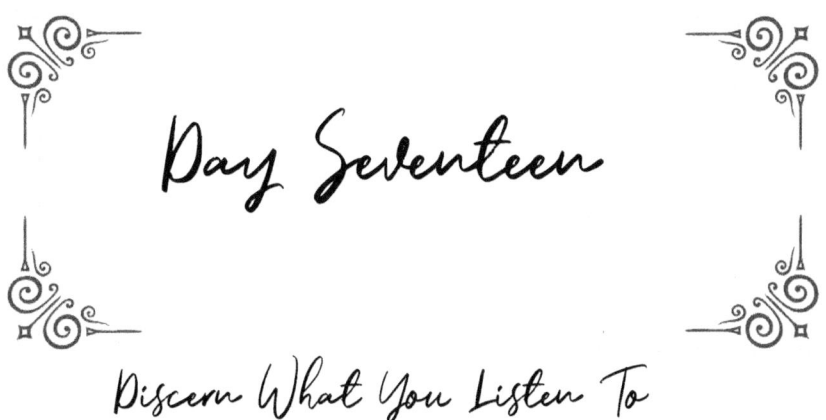

Day Seventeen

Discern What You Listen To

While you are discerning your inner circle you also should be discerning what you are listening to. Are people telling you about the other woman ~ what she looks like; who she is; what is wrong with her; why you are better than her? Why do you need to know this? Yes, you are wanting to know why he went to her when he had you. However, this information is feeding your pain and anger, not helping you to heal. Does knowing all about her, when they were together and where they were seen together matter at this point? The answer is NO. It happened and it is time to move forward.

Secondly, if the people feeding you the information knew all of this, why did they not speak up before it went too far or got to this point? Why did they not advise your spouse he was doing wrong? Why did they not come to you before now?

Knowing these things does not allow you to go back and change anything. You are no better than her and she is no better than you. Let it go and give it to God. When people start feeding you this type of information, politely tell them you are not interested.

Trust me, I listened to the information and all it did was fuel my anger. It also caused me to wonder about the people telling me the information. Were they really my friends? Why did they not do something? So, no, do not listen to negative information and details that do not matter at this point. Read your bible. Pray, and talk to God. He will not tell you anything you do not need to hear.

Scriptures

"But there were also false prophets among the people, just as there will be false teachers among you. They will secretly introduce destructive heresies, even denying the sovereign Lord who bought them—bringing swift destruction on themselves. Many will follow their depraved conduct and will bring the way of truth into disrepute. In their greed these teachers will exploit you with fabricated stories. Their condemnation has long been hanging over them, and their destruction has not been sleeping". ~ **2 Peter 2:1-3**

"Dear friends, do not believe every spirit, but test the spirits to see whether they are from God, because many false prophets have gone out into the world. This is how you can recognize the Spirit of God: Every spirit that acknowledges that Jesus Christ has come in the flesh is from God, but every spirit that does not acknowledge Jesus is not from God. This is the spirit of the antichrist, which you have heard is coming and even now is already in the world. You, dear children, are from God and have overcome them, because the one who is in you is greater than the one who is in the world. They are from the world and therefore speak from the viewpoint of the world, and the world listens to them. We are from God, and whoever knows God listens to us; but whoever is not from God does not listen to us. This is how we recognize the Spirit of truth and the spirit of falsehood". ~ **1 John 4:1-6**

"Refrain from anger and turn from wrath; do not fret—it leads only to evil. For those who are evil will be destroyed, but those who hope in the Lord will inherit the land". ~ **Psalm 37:8-9**

"Then Peter began to speak: "I now realize how true it is that God does not show favoritism but accepts from every nation the one who fears Him and does what is right". ~ **Acts 10:34**

Gina Erwin

Prayer

Dear God,

Help me discern what I listen to and help me not to feel less than the woman You made me to be. I know I am not better than her and she is not better than me. I do not need to know all the intricate details to move forward. All that information will do is heat up my anger and allow the influence of the devil in my life. God strengthen me please. Hold me when I do not feel adequate and remind me, I am your daughter, wonderfully made. God forgive those bringing me this unnecessary information, they think they are helping me when in fact they are not. Guide me forward and assist me in letting it go and giving it all over to You. Thank You, God for loving me and giving me the wisdom and understanding to move forward.

"In the Mighty Name of Jesus"
Amen

My Journal

Date: _____

_____
_____
_____
_____
_____
_____
_____
_____
_____
_____
_____
_____

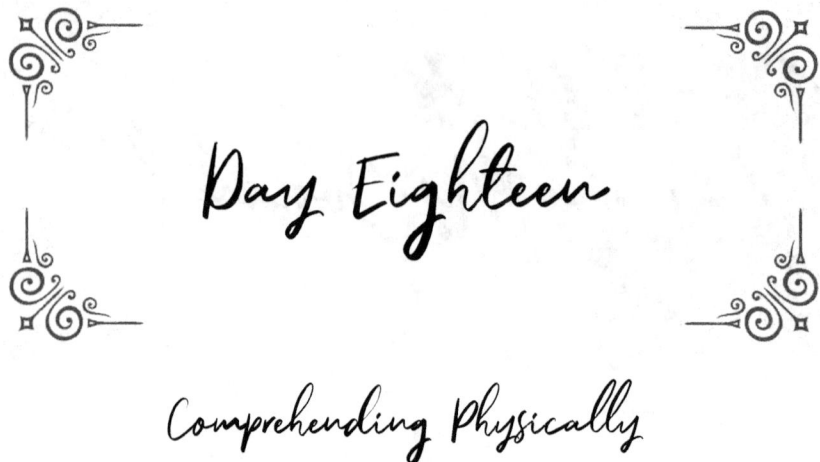

Day Eighteen

Comprehending Physically

To comprehend something means to understand what it is and why it is happening. Some people feel actual pain from adultery. How is this possible? Your heart is the core of your being and when it hurts you can feel physical pain. You are overwhelmed right now causing you to feel worn out and tired. Your anger is up, and it can make your blood pressure rise causing physical symptoms. You may be depressed which causes physical changes in your body. It is possible for adultery to affect you physically, so, do not be surprised if it does. Your body is made of flesh and your flesh is weak, making it easily affected.

Here is where God comes in. God is a spirit and can heal you and upbuild your spirit which in turn can and will upbuild your body if you let it. You must trust God, pray, and know that He will help you. Do not give in to the physical pain and let it overtake you. Call on your help, God. Now if you are experiencing severe or pain that insinuates something is physically wrong, consult a physician. Otherwise consult and trust in the Great Physician, God.

This pain too shall pass as all the other negative aspects of the situation will in time. Trusting God and loving yourself is what you must do. When you absolutely love yourself and trust God it is easy to submit to His will and

Scriptures

"Therefore, we do not lose heart. Though outwardly we are wasting away, yet inwardly we are being renewed day by day. For our light and momentary troubles are achieving for us an eternal glory that far outweighs them all. So, we fix our eyes not on what is seen, but on what is unseen, since what is seen is temporary, but what is unseen is eternal".
~ **2 Corinthians 4:16-18**

"Humble yourselves, therefore, under God's mighty hand, that he may lift you up in due time. Cast all your anxiety on Him because he cares for you. Be alert and of sober mind. Your enemy the devil prowls around like a roaring lion looking for someone to devour. Resist Him, standing firm in the faith, because you know that the family of believers throughout the world is undergoing the same kind of sufferings. And the God of all grace, who called you to His eternal glory in Christ, after you have suffered a little while, will Himself restore you and make you strong, firm and steadfast. To Him be the power for ever and ever. Amen". ~ **1 Peter 5:6-11**

"My son, pay attention to what I say; turn your ear to my words. Do not let them out of your sight, keep them within your heart; for they are life to those who find them and health to one's whole body. Above all else, guard your heart, for everything you do flows from it". ~ **Proverbs 4:20-23**

"A happy heart makes the face cheerful, but heartache crushes the spirit".
~ **Proverbs 15:13**

Gina Erwin

Prayer

Dear Father in Heaven,
My heart hurts. I am feeling physical pain from this situation. I am so hurt right now that I am not sure what is right and what is wrong. You are a spirit and I ask You to strengthen my spirit so I can heal, and my heart can heal too. God remove this pain and guide me forward. Help me stand with all the madness going on around me. Help me. Heal me. Love me. Thank You for all You do for me and give to me. This too shall pass if I trust and rely on You.

In Jesus' Name,
Amen

Putting the Pieces Back Together After Divorce

My Journal

Date: _____

107

Day Nineteen

Comprehending Mentally

Now that we have dealt with the physical, we need to address the mental aspect of the situation and what is going on in your mind. More than likely, all kinds of thoughts are circling inside your mind. You are thinking about your spouse, what you had, what he did, what you could have had, and wondering where you go from here. Your mind is in overdrive and that can also affect you physically. You can feel exhausted and drained. You may even be wondering what people are thinking and saying about you.

What you must know is that all that matters are what God thinks and feels about you and the situation. You must keep your mind on God, His will, and the right moves to make going forward. You do not have to please man, you must please God. This is a deep core situation and makes it easier to want the wrong things. You must focus your mind on God and what you need to do, not the other woman, or why it happened. You must control your thoughts to take the right actions. This means keeping God's word in your heart and mind always. Read your bible. Proverbs is an excellent book for this. It gives you the bases for how God wants you to act in accordance with His will. Also, there are stories such as David and Bathsheba found in 2 Samuel chapters 11 and 12 and Delilah's betrayal of Samson at Judges chapter 16. The bible is full of everyday situations, making God's will clear in them all. Reading the bible will occupy your mind and overtake those wondering thoughts and ideas. Also pray and ask God to guide and show you what you need to know, hear, and see.

Scriptures

"Those who live according to the flesh have their minds set on what the flesh desires; but those who live in accordance with the Spirit have their minds set on what the Spirit desires. The mind governed by the flesh is death, but the mind governed by the Spirit is life and peace. The mind governed by the flesh is hostile to God; it does not submit to God's law, nor can it do so. Those who are in the realm of the flesh cannot please God. You, however, are not in the realm of the flesh but are in the realm of the Spirit, if indeed the Spirit of God lives in you. And if anyone does not have the Spirit of Christ, they do not belong to Christ. But if Christ is in you, then even though your body is subject to death because of sin, the Spirit gives life because of righteousness. And if the Spirit of Him who raised Jesus from the dead is living in you, he who raised Christ from the dead will also give life to your mortal bodies because of His Spirit who lives in you." ~ **Romans 8:5-11**

"Your eyes will see strange sights, and your mind will imagine confusing things. You will be like one sleeping on the high seas, lying on top of the rigging. "They hit me", you will say, "but I'm not hurt! They beat me, but I don't feel it!" ~ **Proverbs 23:33-35**

"Do your best to present yourself to God as one approved, a worker who does not need to be ashamed and who correctly handles the word of truth. Avoid Godless chatter because those who indulge in it will become more and more ungodly". ~ **2 Timothy 2:15-16**

"All Scripture is God-breathed and is useful for teaching, rebuking, correcting and training in righteousness, so that the servant of God may be thoroughly equipped for every good work". ~ **2 Timothy 3:16**

Prayer

God in Heaven Above,

Guide me to You and Your Word. Allow Your Words to enter my mind and heart, so I understand what You require of me and want me to do. Allow Your word to infiltrate my negative thoughts and prevent me from making wrong choices and acting in a manner unpleasing to You. Allow me to receive Your instruction and guidance. Give me the wisdom and understanding I require as well as the strength and determination to do what is right in Your sight. Thank You for giving us Your Word as a manual to live by.

In Jesus' Name,
Amen

My Journal

Date: _____

Day Twenty
Comprehending Spiritually

Comprehending spiritually means knowing the difference between the spirit and the flesh and acting accordingly to the spirit of God and not your own flesh. It is easy to act according to the flesh. It takes work and determination to act according to the spirit of God. God is a spirit and His spirit interact with ours through the Holy Spirit.

First and foremost, you must get in line with God to communicate and understand His plans for you, what He expects from you, and what moves you should or should not make.

Next, you also must realize that your and your spouse's spirits were connected and bonded, so you are feeling a break in that bond. It is like losing a loved one. You feel an internal loss. This area will help you in determining which path to take, while staying in accordance with God's will and your vows. While adultery is biblical grounds for divorce, that does not mean it is the path you should take.

You need to be in touch with your spirit and let it communicate with God. This is the way to true healing and making the correct decisions moving forward. What may be right for someone else, is not necessarily the path for you. You need to understand how your spirit feels and what God wants you to do.

Scriptures

"Haven't you read," he replied, "that at the beginning the Creator 'made them male and female,' and said, 'For this reason a man will leave His father and mother and be united to His wife, and the two will become **one flesh**'? So, they are no longer two, but one flesh. Therefore, what God has joined together, let no one separate". ~ **Matthew 19:4~6**

"The wife does not have authority over her own body but yields it to her husband. In the same way, the husband does not have authority over His own body but yields it to His wife". ~ **1 Corinthians 7:4**

"Place me like a seal over your heart, like a seal on your arm; for **love is as strong as death**, its jealousy unyielding as the grave. It burns like blazing fire, like a mighty flame. Many waters cannot quench love; rivers cannot sweep it away. If one were to give all the wealth of one's house for love, it would be utterly scorned". ~ **Song of Songs 8:6~7**

"Yet a time is coming and has now come when the true worshipers will worship the Father in the Spirit and in truth, for they are the kind of worshipers the Father seeks. God is spirit, and His worshipers must worship in the Spirit and in truth". ~
John 4:23~24

"But when he, the Spirit of truth, comes, he will guide you into all the truth. He will not speak on His own; he will speak only what he hears, and he will tell you what is yet to come. He will glorify me because it is from me that he will receive what he will make known to you. All that belongs to the Father is mine. That is why I said the Spirit will receive from me what he will make known to you". ~ **John 16:13~15**

"But we ought always to thank God for you, brothers and sisters loved by the Lord, because God chose you as first fruits to be saved through the sanctifying work of the Spirit and through belief in the truth. He called you to this through our gospel, that you might share in the glory of our Lord Jesus Christ. So then, brothers and sisters, stand firm and hold fast to the teachings we passed on to you, whether by word of mouth or by letter. May our Lord Jesus Christ Himself and God our Father, who loved us and by His grace gave us eternal encouragement and good hope, encourage your hearts and strengthen you in every good deed and word". ~ **2 Thessalonians 2:13~17**

"The eyes of the Lord are on the righteous, and His ears are attentive to their cry; but the face of the Lord is against those who do evil, to blot out their name from the earth. The righteous cry out, and the Lord hears them; he delivers them from all their troubles. The Lord is close to the brokenhearted and saves those who are crushed in spirit. The righteous person may have many troubles, but the Lord delivers Him from them all; he protects all His bones, not one of them will be broken". ~ **Psalm 34:15~20**

Gina Erwin

Prayer

Dear God,

I come to You in spirit and truth. I need your guidance and wisdom. The actions of my spouse have caused me to be at a loss of both understanding and spiritual connection with Him. Help me to reach out to You in my time of need and allow my spirit to be guided by You as it leads me to the path You want me to take. Only You know what I need and what is next for me. I am not sure of anything except You right now God. Hold me, guide me, and poor your spirit out on me. God, I thank You for all You have in store for me and my future as I walk in your purpose and will. Thank You for your love, kindness, mercy, and grace.

In Jesus' Name
Amen

Putting the Pieces Back Together After Divorce

Date: _____

_____
_____
_____
_____
_____
_____
_____
_____
_____
_____
_____
_____

Day Twenty-One

Comprehending Financially

What does finances have to do with this? In making your decisions moving forward, your financial situation must be evaluated and understood. Do you work? Is this a two-income household or a one? Whom is the primary wage earner? If you choose to separate and/or divorce, do you have the means to support yourself and any children?

You need to comprehend these issues to move forward without placing yourself in dire straits. Not to say you should remain in a marriage for monetary reasons, you just need to know how to proceed forward making sure you and your children have what you need with or without your spouse.

If you separate will you need to find employment? What are your qualifications? Do you need to go back to school for added training? Finances is a necessity in your moving forward. It is also vital to your continued success.

Pray to God to provide for you and your family. Know what you need to do moving forward. Be aware of your finances. Do not fear because God will provide if you are in accordance with Him. However, be aware and be smart in your actions.

Scriptures

"Wisdom has built her house; she has set up its seven pillars. She has prepared her meat and mixed her wine; she has also set her table". ~ **Proverbs 9:1~2**

"Preach the word; be prepared in season and out of season; correct, rebuke and encourage - with great patience and careful instruction". ~ **2 Timothy 4:2**

"Wisdom, like an inheritance, is a good thing and benefits those who see the sun. Wisdom is a shelter as money is a shelter, but the advantage of knowledge is this: Wisdom preserves those who have it". ~ **Ecclesiastes 7:11~12**

"Dishonest money dwindles away, but whoever gathers money little by little makes it grow". ~ **Proverbs 13~11**

"But Godliness with contentment is great gain. For we brought nothing into the world, and we can take nothing out of it. But if we have food and clothing, we will be content with that. Those who want to get rich fall into temptation and a trap and into many foolish and harmful desires that plunge people into ruin and destruction. For the love of money is a root of all kinds of evil. Some people, eager for money, have wandered from the faith and pierced themselves with many griefs". ~ **1 Timothy 6:6~10**

"And my God will meet all your needs according to the riches of His glory in Christ Jesus". ~ **Philippians 4:19**

Gina Erwin

Prayer

Dear God,

Please help me use wisdom when spending money now and in the future. Do not allow me to worship money but use it to sustain and support my family. Help me be aware of how money needs affect this situation, moving forward, and making decisions. Thank You, God for taking care of me and supplying my needs now and in the future.

In Jesus' Name
Amen!

My Journal

Date: _____

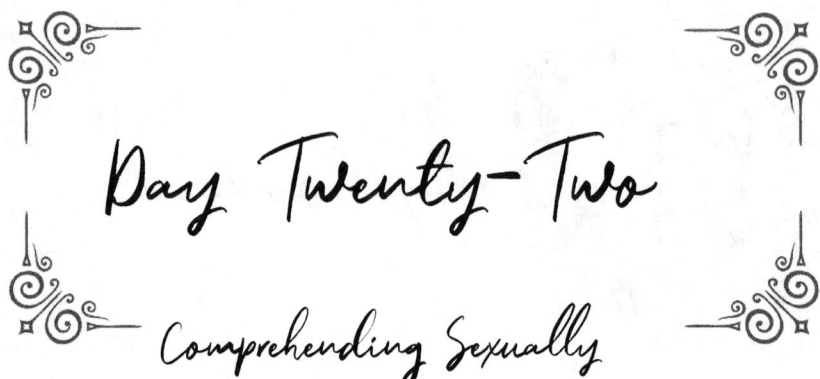

Day Twenty-Two
Comprehending Sexually

Sex? You may be thinking, what do you have to comprehend about sex? Is sex not why this situation occurred in the first place? Sex is probably the last thing you want to think about right now. However, it must be addressed.

A lack of sex within the marriage bed may have a direct affect that led to this situation. Also, when deciding on your future path, you must understand your feelings and needs in the sexual aspect. By this I mean, if you choose to divorce, going out and having sex with another man is not in accord with God's will. Staying with your spouse and choosing to work it out and not having sex with Him is also not following God's will. Therefore, knowing your sexual habits and needs does play a vital role in the decision-making process.

Sex is a part of marriage. Sex is not a sin. It did not get Adam and Eve thrown out of the Garden of Eden or cause imperfection and death. That was disobedience. We were created out of loved, to be loved, and to share the intimacy of sex with our spouses. Sex is also the way we are fruitful and multiply as directed by God. Sex is not dirty, forbidden, or a sin, unless it is used in a perverted manner other than what God intended.

So, moving forward understand and comprehend your sexual behavior and needs as you consider what actions to take moving forward. Remember this is just one aspect needing to be understood before decision-making and in keeping yourself in

God's will

Putting the Pieces Back Together After Divorce

Scriptures

"Adam made love to His wife Eve, and she became pregnant and gave birth to Cain. She said, "With the help of the Lord I have brought forth a man". ~ **Genesis 4:1**

"So, the Lord God caused the man to fall into a deep sleep; and while he was sleeping, he took one of the man's ribs and then closed up the place with flesh. Then the Lord God made a woman from the rib he had taken out of the man, and he brought her to the man. The man said, "This is now bone of my bones and flesh of my flesh; she shall be called 'woman', for she was taken out of man". That is why a man leaves His father and mother and is united to His wife, and they become one flesh.
Adam and His wife were both naked, and they felt no shame". ~ **Genesis 2:21~24**

"Now for the matters you wrote about: "It is good for a man not to have sexual relations with a woman". But since sexual immorality is occurring, each man should have sexual relations with His own wife, and each woman with her own husband. The husband should fulfill His marital duty to His wife, and likewise the wife to her husband. The wife does not have authority over her own body but yields it to her husband. In the same way, the husband does not have authority over His own body but yields it to His wife. Do not deprive each other except perhaps by mutual consent and for a time, so that you may devote yourselves to prayer. Then come together again so that Satan will not tempt you because of your lack of self-control. I say this as a concession, not as a command. I wish that all of you were as I am. But each of you has your own gift from God; one has this gift, another has that. Now to the unmarried and the widows I say: It is good for them to stay unmarried, as I do. But if they cannot control themselves, they should marry, for it is better to marry than to burn with passion". ~ **1 Corinthians 7:1~9**

Gina Erwin

Prayer

My Creator,

I come before you, asking that You to help me see this situation from all angles including sexually. Sex is a part of marriage and the main topic of this situation. Help me understand my needs and desires and incorporate them in moving forward and making future decisions. I want to remain in your will and do all You want me to. Please allow me to remain true to You now and in the future. Guide me to the right decisions God. Thank you for the gift of marriage and the good times I have shared with my spouse. Thank You for helping me focus on what is right and not the pain and hurt. Thank You, God, for all You have planned for my future.

In Jesus' Name,
Amen

Putting the Pieces Back Together After Divorce

Date: _____

_____
_____
_____
_____
_____
_____
_____
_____
_____
_____
_____
_____

Day Twenty-Three

Dealing with Your Emotions

Emotions are unlimited and will come and go both slowly and quickly depending on you and what you focus on. There is anger, hurt, desiring revenge, sadness, sorrow, defeat, and many more emotions you will experience in this situation. What you must do is focus on moving forward and avoiding the emotions that will remove you from God's will. God's word tells us which emotions are of God and which are not. Yes, your spouse was wrong for committing adultery, but you must not allow yourself to focus on negative emotions such as anger and hurt which lead to desiring revenge. You will feel sorrow and sadness which will cause God to draw closer to help you. You may even feel defeated and due to the situation, it is understandable, but you must not give up. You must move forward trusting in God to make it better and help you move forward in truth and love.

Do not let your emotions cause you to give up on love because God is love and you must love to be in God's will. Love did not cause this pain and should not be cast aside and avoided.

Be aware of your emotions and feelings. Do your best to avoid negative thoughts and emotions. When it becomes overwhelming, pray to God for help. He is there for you.

Scriptures

"The acts of the flesh are obvious: sexual immorality, impurity and debauchery; idolatry and witchcraft; hatred, discord, jealousy, fits of rage, selfish ambition, dissensions, factions and envy; drunkenness, orgies, and the like. I warn you, as I did before, that those who live like this will not inherit the kingdom of God. But the fruit of the Spirit is love, joy, peace, forbearance, kindness, goodness, faithfulness, gentleness, and self-control. Against such things there is no law. Those who belong to Christ Jesus have crucified the flesh with its passions and desires. Since we live by the Spirit, let us keep in step with the Spirit. Let us not become conceited, provoking and envying each other". ~ **Galatians 5:19~26**

"Blessed are the poor in spirit, for theirs is the kingdom of heaven. Blessed are those who mourn, for they will be comforted. Blessed are the meek, for they will inherit the earth. Blessed are those who hunger and thirst for righteousness, for they will be filled. Blessed are the merciful, for they will be shown mercy. Blessed are the pure in heart, for they will see God. Blessed are the peacemakers, for they will be called children of God. Blessed are those who are persecuted because of righteousness, for theirs is the kingdom of heaven. "Blessed are you when people insult you, persecute you and falsely say all kinds of evil against you because of me. Rejoice and be glad, because great is your reward in heaven, for in the same way they persecuted the prophets who were before you". ~ **Matthew 5:3~12**

"If I speak in the tongues of men or of angels, but do not have love, I am only a resounding gong or a clanging cymbal. If I have the gift of prophecy and can fathom all mysteries and all knowledge, and if I have a faith that can move mountains, but do not have love, I am nothing. If I give all I possess to the poor and give over my body to hardship that I may boast, but do not have love, I gain nothing. Love is patient, love is kind. It does not envy, it does not boast, it is not proud. It does not dishonor others, it is not self-seeking, it is not easily angered, it keeps no record of wrongs. Love does not delight in evil but rejoices with the truth. It always protects, always trusts, always hopes, always perseveres. Love never fails. But where there are prophecies, they will cease; where there are tongues, they will be stilled; where there is knowledge, it will pass away. For we know in part and we prophesy in part, but when completeness comes, what is in part disappears. When I was a child, I talked like a child, I thought like a child, I reasoned like a child. When I became a man, I put the ways of childhood behind me. For now, we see only a reflection as in a mirror; then we shall see face to face. Now I know in part; then I shall know fully, even as I am fully known. And now these three remain: faith, hope, and love. But the greatest of these is love". ~ **1 Corinthians 13:1~13**

"I will instruct you and teach you in the way you should go; I will counsel you with my loving eye on you. Do not be like the horse or the mule, which have no understanding but must be controlled by bit and bridle or they will not come to you. Many are the woes of the wicked, but the Lord's unfailing love surrounds the one who trusts in Him. Rejoice in the Lord and be glad, you righteous; sing, all you who are upright in heart!" ~ **Psalm 32:8~11**

"A person is praised according to their prudence, and one with a warped mind is despised". ~ **Proverbs 12:8**

"Lord, who may dwell in your sacred tent? Who may live on your holy mountain? The one whose walk is blameless, who does what is righteous, who speaks the truth from their heart; whose tongue utters no slander, who does no wrong to a neighbor, and casts no slur on others; who despises a vile person but honors those who fear the Lord; who keeps an oath even when it hurts, and does not change their mind; who lends money to the poor without interest; who does not accept a bribe against the innocent. Whoever does these things will never be shaken". ~ **Psalm 15:1~5**

"Do not repay anyone evil for evil. Be careful to do what is right in the eyes of everyone. If it is possible, as far as it depends on you, live at peace with everyone. Do not take revenge, my dear friends, but leave room for God's wrath, for it is written: "It is mine to avenge; I will repay", says the Lord." ~ **Romans 12:17~19**

Gina Erwin

Prayer

Dear God,

My emotions are all over the place. One minute I feel **(State your feeling)**, and the next I feel **(State your feeling)**. I want to focus on doing what is right in your sight God and not on what my flesh is feeling. Please God help me to control my mind, thoughts, and desires. Do not allow my pain to overtake me and cause me to go against your will. Pour your spirit out on me God and guide me forward in your will. Thank You, God I love You and need You. Thank You for loving me even when I do not deserve it. God hold me close and keep me safe. Thank You, God for all You do and all You will do.

In Jesus' Name,
Amen

Putting the Pieces Back Together After Divorce

Date: _____

_____

_____

_____

_____

_____

_____

_____

_____

_____

_____

_____

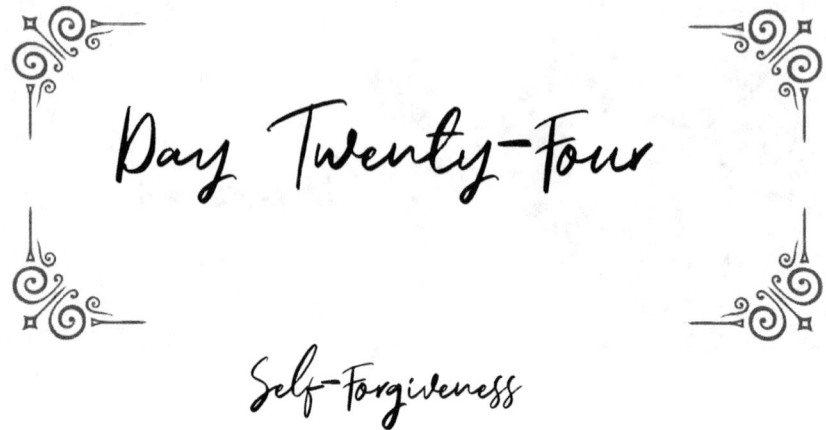

Day Twenty-Four

Self-Forgiveness

Forgiveness is something that must occur in all areas of life and especially in adultery. To be forgiven of our sins, we must forgive others when they sin against us. There are three primary areas of forgiveness with adultery, self-forgiveness, forgiveness of all others involved in the situation, and forgiveness of your mate.

First let us look at self-forgiveness. You may be asking yourself, "What did I do wrong?", "Did he leave because I was supportive enough?", "Was I not good enough?", or "What could I have done to prevent this?". You may be feeling responsible or blaming yourself. It is not anyone's fault. It is a combination of wrong decisions. You must know that this is not your fault even if you made mistakes.

You must forgive yourself for any responsibility you have placed on yourself and ask God to forgive you as well. Once you sincerely ask God to forgive you, He does. It is you yourself that must let it go. You are not perfect, and you could have made mistakes, but IT IS NOT YOUR FAULT! It has happened and the time has come to face it and move forward. You cannot move forward until you forgive yourself.

Look at your whole life. Yes, you have made wrong choices and mistakes. We all have and do daily. We are all imperfect. Through forgiveness and the love of God, you can be made whole again. Do not just look at this situation, look deep within yourself and see what you are feeling. Use this time to communicate with yourself. There may be issues from your past you have not dealt with and are feeling guilty about. It is time to work on yourself so that whatever decisions you make moving forward will only build you and all concerned up, not cause additional conflicts. You need to be okay with and love yourself.

Once you have forgiven yourself for everything that you have kept bottled up for however long, your mind is clearer, and you can communicate with God and begin to forgive the others involved, including your spouse.

Self-forgiveness is most often harder than forgiving others. We are harder on ourselves than anyone else. It starts with you. You are God's daughter, loved by Him, and you will overcome this with His help. Forgive yourself for all things.

Scriptures

"For this reason, since the day we heard about you, we have not stopped praying for you. We continually ask God to fill you with the knowledge of His will through all the wisdom and understanding that the Spirit gives, so that you may live a life worthy of the Lord and please Him in every way: bearing fruit in every good work, growing in the knowledge of God, being strengthened with all power according to His glorious might so that you may have great endurance and patience, and giving joyful thanks to the Father, who has qualified you to share in the inheritance of His holy people in the kingdom of light. For he has rescued us from the dominion of darkness and brought us into the kingdom of the Son he loves, in whom we have redemption, the forgiveness of sins". ~ **Colossians 1:9~14**

"This is the message we have heard from Him and declare to you: God is light; in Him there is no darkness at all. If we claim to have fellowship with Him and yet walk in the darkness, we lie and do not live out the truth. But if we walk in the light, as he is in the light, we have fellowship with one another, and the blood of Jesus, His Son, purifies us from all sin. If we claim to be without sin, we deceive ourselves and the truth is not in us. If we confess our sins, he is faithful and just and will forgive us our sins and purify us from all unrighteousness. If we claim we have not sinned, we make Him out to be a liar and His word is not in us". ~ **1 John 1:5~10**

"But who can discern their own errors? Forgive my hidden faults". ~ **Psalm 19:12**

"Good and upright is the Lord; therefore, he instructs sinners in His ways. He guides the humble in what is right and teaches them His way. All the ways of the Lord are loving and faithful toward those who keep the demands of His covenant. For the sake of your name, Lord, forgive my iniquity, though it is great". ~ **Psalm 25:8~11**

"Blessed is the one whose transgressions are forgiven, whose sins are covered. Blessed is the one whose sin the Lord does not count against them and in whose spirit, is no deceit. When I kept silent, my bones wasted away through my groaning all day long. For day and night your hand was heavy on me; my strength was sapped as in the heat of summer. Then I acknowledged my sin to you and did not cover up my iniquity. I said, "I will confess my transgressions to the Lord". And you forgave the guilt of my sin". ~ **Psalm 32:1~5**

"Is anyone among you in trouble? Let them pray. Is anyone happy? Let them sing songs of praise. Is anyone among you sick? Let them call the elders of the church to pray over them and anoint them with oil in the name of the Lord. And the prayer offered in faith will make the sick person well; the Lord will raise them up. If they have sinned, they will be forgiven. Therefore, confess your sins to each other and pray for each other so that you may be healed. The prayer of a righteous person is powerful and effective". ~ **James 5:13~16**

Gina Erwin

Prayer

Dear God,

I am not perfect and have made many mistakes. God please forgive me and help me to forgive myself. If you can forgive me, then I know through prayer and communication with you I can let go and forgive myself. Help me see what you see in me and know that I am worth it God. Help me love myself, so I can in turn love You and others the way they deserve to be loved. Help me love myself so others too can love me. God thank you for creating me in your image and giving me the ability to show, give, and experience love.

In the Mighty Name of Your Son, Jesus.
Amen

Putting the Pieces Back Together After Divorce

Date: _____

_____
_____
_____
_____
_____
_____
_____
_____
_____
_____
_____
_____
_____

Day Twenty-Five

Forgiveness of All Individuals Involved

A great injustice has been committed against you. However, you must forgive all involved. This means the other woman and all who were aware of the situation whether they tried to stop it or not. Forgiveness does not mean you must deal with them, but God's word says you must forgive and love them. I said love, not be best friends. When you love someone, you want what is best for them and do not wish harm to come to them. So, in forgiving all those concerned, you must let it go so it does not keep reentering your thoughts and causing discord. Yes, you were hurt by their actions, lack of action, and/or their knowledge of the situation. However, you must forgive them because God requires it, they need it, it will clear you, and you must forgive to be forgiven.

When we hold grudges and do not forgive, the individuals we are upset with have a hold on us. Have you ever been upset with someone, hurt by them, not forgiven them, and run into them? Your whole demeaner will change and you will go from being content to hateful or upset. No one should have that type of control over you except for God Himself. By forgiving and giving the situation to God, you in return free yourself. You release yourself from the burden of holding a grudge. You also gain the ability to be forgiven.

It has happened and there is nothing anyone can do to change it.

It is not your place to be judge and jury. That is God's place and responsibility. Everyone must move forward knowing the roles they played in the situation. Once you forgive, you can deal with the situation in a Godly manner, not out of spite or other inappropriate emotions. Forgive them and free yourself. Move forward in the purpose God has for you, not being sidetracked by unforgiveness.

You have so much more to do and consider than being unforgiving and desiring revenge. Let go and let God. He has the power and authority, not you. You have major decisions to make about your marriage and the future of your family. To do this accurately, in the best manner, and in accord with God's will you have to be clearheaded and in a calm space.

You must set the example for all involved. If you have children, you must show them you are doing things God's way. They are being affected and your behavior can help or hinder them. Be mindful of everyone, your family, friends, and everyone else.

I remember losing it when I found out. I felt like someone had stabbed me with a knife. I was talked down to by the other woman and had a friend relay everything to me. I felt disrespected and wanted everyone to hurt like I was hurting. Truthfully all my friend knew and told me showed she was not just aware but running in the same circles as they were. It took a lot for me to forgive, but I did it for me and my family. My children and best friend were spending all their time comforting me and trying to help me get through. When I finally could give it to God and forgive them, I found the peace I longed for. Not only did I gain peace, my whole household did.

Forgiveness is for your benefit. Do not let them have any hold or control over you because you will not forgive them. Take control and forgive. Do it for God and yourself.

Scriptures

"Jesus said, "Father, forgive them, for they do not know what they are doing."" ~ **Luke 23:34**

"For if you forgive other people when they sin against you, your heavenly Father will also forgive you. But if you do not forgive others their sins, your Father will not forgive your sins". ~ **Matthew 6:14~15**

"Then Peter came to Jesus and asked, "Lord, how many times shall I forgive my brother or sister who sins against me? Up to seven times?" Jesus answered, "I tell you, not seven times, but seventy-seven times. "~ **Matthew 18:21~22**

So, watch yourselves. "If your brother or sister sins against you, rebuke them; and if they repent, forgive them. Even if they sin against you seven times in a day and seven times come back to you saying, 'I repent', you must forgive them". The apostles said to the Lord, "Increase our faith!" He replied, "If you have faith as small as a mustard seed, you can say to this mulberry tree, 'Be uprooted and planted in the sea,' and it will obey you." ~ **Luke 17:3~6**

"If anyone has caused grief, he has not so much grieved me as he has grieved all of you to some extent—not to put it too severely. The punishment inflicted on Him by the majority is sufficient.
Now instead, you ought to forgive and comfort Him, so that he will not be overwhelmed by excessive sorrow. I urge you, therefore, to reaffirm your love for Him. Another reason I wrote you was to see if you would stand the test and be obedient in everything. Anyone you forgive, I also forgive. And what I have forgiven - if there was anything to forgive - I have forgiven in the sight of Christ for your sake, in order that Satan

might not outwit us. For we are not unaware of His schemes". ~ **2 Corinthians 2:5~11**

"Therefore, as God's chosen people, holy and dearly loved, clothe yourselves with compassion, kindness, humility, gentleness and patience. Bear with each other and forgive one another if any of you has a grievance against someone. Forgive as the Lord forgave you. And over all these virtues put on love, which binds them all together in perfect unity. Let the peace of Christ rule in your hearts, since as members of one body you were called to peace. And be thankful. Let the message of Christ dwell among you richly as you teach and admonish one another with all wisdom through psalms, hymns, and songs from the Spirit, singing to God with gratitude in your hearts. And whatever you do, whether in word or deed, do it all in the name of the Lord Jesus, giving thanks to God the Father through Him". ~ **Colossians 3:12~17**

Gina Erwin

Prayer

Father God,

Help me to forgive all the people involved in and that played roles in this situation. Help me to let go of the hurt and anger and give the situation to you. I am angry, hurt, and **(state your feelings)**. God help me let it go and remove it from my heart, mind, and soul. Take this burden and allow me to forgive. Show me what to do God and how to do it. Help me to free myself so I can move forward in Your will. Into Your hands I give it all God. I release it all to You. God thank You for loving me. Thank You for showing me the right path to take. Thank You for all You are doing and will do in working out this situation. Thank You for forgiving me.

In Jesus' Name,
Amen!

Putting the Pieces Back Together After Divorce

Date: _____

_____
_____
_____
_____
_____
_____
_____
_____
_____
_____
_____
_____

Day Twenty-Six

Forgiveness of Your Mate

Now to the big forgiveness. Yes, you can forgive your spouse. You may not want to but again, you must. You must regain and be in control of yourself, your decisions, and your actions. You must be in control to willingly do things in accord with God's will.

You loved this man and if it was true Godly love, you still do, whether you want to or not. This was one of the hardest things for me to understand. Once, I truly gave it to God and forgave my husband, I realized that I still loved Him. In all honesty, I did not want to still love Him because it would be easier if I did not care.

Love is a gift from God and God is love. We fall short and hurt God daily, yet He still loves us and does not give up on us. My true love for my husband allowed me to still love Him once I forgave His actions. It freed me from feelings that are not of
God.

When hatred, a work of the flesh, prevails we are not living in truth. When we forgive, allow God, and continue to love everyone, we are. My truth was I still loved Him. Though we are separated I did forgive Him and still love Him. I pray for Him every night and ask God to protect and take care of Him.

This is an example of forgiveness and God's "agape" love. The devil does not want us to love in this way, because it draws us closer to God.

Yes, we must cope with the pain and hurt, but God will restore you in His time.

Just as there is a thin line between love and hate, there is even a thinner line between God and the devil. Which side do you want to be on? The devil does not want us to love. He wants us to live against all of God's principles. If the devil tempted Jesus, why would he not tempt us. This situation is the perfect scenario for the devil to come in if you are not careful.

It was not all bad. There were good times. You had a loving relationship. Things have changed, but do not let the devil use the bad to outweigh the good. Trust me, he will if you let Him.

Forgive your spouse, free yourself, and free Him. By doing this you can make decisions that God wants you to make and that are best for you and all concerned. Forgiving Him will allow you both to come to a place where you can at least communicate, whether you decide to remain together or not.

Scriptures

"Love is patient, love is kind. It does not envy, it does not boast, it is not proud. It does not dishonor others, it is not self-seeking, it is not easily angered, it keeps no record of wrongs. Love does not delight in evil but rejoices with the truth. It always protects, always trusts, always hopes, always perseveres. Love never fails". ~ **1 Corinthians 13:4~8**

"But now apart from the law the righteousness of God has been made known, to which the Law and the Prophets testify. This righteousness is given through faith in Jesus Christ to all who believe. There is no difference between Jew and Gentile, for all have sinned and fall short of the glory of God, and all are justified freely by His grace through the redemption that came by Christ Jesus". ~ **Romans 3:21~24**

"Marriage should be honored by all, and the marriage bed kept pure, for God will judge the adulterer and all the sexually immoral. Keep your lives free from the love of money and be content with what you have, because God has said, "Never will I leave you; never will I forsake you". So, we say with confidence, "The Lord is my helper; I will not be afraid. What can mere mortals do to me?"" ~ **Hebrews 13:4~6**

"The acts of the flesh are obvious: sexual immorality, impurity and debauchery; idolatry and witchcraft; hatred, discord, jealousy, fits of rage, selfish ambition, dissensions, factions and envy; drunkenness, orgies, and the like. I warn you, as I did before, that those who live like this will not inherit the kingdom of God. But the fruit of the Spirit is love, joy, peace, forbearance, kindness, goodness, faithfulness, gentleness, and self-control. Against such things there is no law. Those who belong to Christ Jesus have crucified the flesh with its passions and desires. Since we live by the Spirit, let us keep in step with the Spirit. Let us not become conceited, provoking and envying each other". ~ **Galatians 5:19~26**

"Humble yourselves, therefore, under God's mighty hand, that he may lift you up in due time. Cast all your anxiety on Him because he cares for you. Be alert and of sober mind. Your enemy the devil prowls around like a roaring lion looking for someone to devour. Resist Him, standing firm in the faith, because you know that the family of believers throughout the world is undergoing the same kind of sufferings. And the God of all grace, who called you to His eternal glory in Christ, after you have suffered a little while, will Himself restore you and make you strong, firm and steadfast. To Him be the power for ever and ever. Amen". ~ **1 Peter 5:6~11**

"Then Jesus was led by the Spirit into the wilderness to be tempted by the devil. After fasting forty days and forty nights, he was hungry. The tempter came to Him and said, "If you are the Son of God, tell these stones to become bread". Jesus answered, "It is written: 'Man shall not live on bread alone, but on every word, that comes from the mouth of God.'" Then the devil took Him to the holy city and had Him stand on the highest point of the temple. "If you are the Son of God", he said, "throw yourself down. For it is written: '"He will command His angels concerning you, and they will lift you up in their hands, so that you will not strike your foot against a stone.'" Jesus answered Him, "It is also written: 'Do not put the Lord your God to the test'" Again, the devil took Him to a very high mountain and showed Him all the kingdoms of the world and their splendor. "All this I will give you", he said, "if you will bow down and worship me". Jesus said to Him, "Away from me, Satan! For it is written: 'Worship the Lord your God and serve Him only.'" Then the devil left Him, and angels came and attended Him". ~ **Matthew 4:1~11**

Gina Erwin

Prayer

Dear God,

Thank You for my husband and all the good times we had. Nothing and no one are perfect except You God. My husband made a wrong choice. Help me to forgive Him and move forward. Help me to see the good in Him and everything else. Help me to do what You want me to. Help me avoid the snare of the devil and not fall for His tricks. Guide me God and help me make the right decisions. Thank You, God for Your love, grace, and wisdom. Thank You for guiding me where You want me to be. I love You, God.

In Jesus' Name,
Amen!

Putting the Pieces Back Together After Divorce

Date: _____

_____
_____
_____
_____
_____
_____
_____
_____
_____
_____

Day Twenty-Seven

Decision-Making

Decision-making is never easy. You must take into consideration all concerned, children, older parents, and anybody else that is a direct part of your family life. If he has children with the other woman, they too must be considered. In making your decision, you must consider God's will along with your physical, emotional, spiritual, mental, financial, and sexual circumstances. You must act out of wisdom and love, not anger and emotion.

This step will be different for everyone reading This book. Your decisions depend on God, you, your spouse, your family, and your specific situation. Some will remain married and get counseling. Some will separate and decide further in the future. Some will divorce. Whatever your decision is, please keep God's will in the forefront and decide from a place of love. The decisions you make will affect you and everyone else concerned.

When you make decisions out of love and in accordance with God's will, you will be able to move forward content, knowing everyone is where they should be and their individual needs are being taken care of. Not only will this bring you peace, it will display your love of God and others. You will reap blessings for your faithfulness.

Scriptures

"My son, do not forget my teaching, but keep my commands in your heart, for they will prolong your life many years and bring you peace and prosperity. Let love and faithfulness never leave you; bind them around your neck, write them on the tablet of your heart. Then you will win favor and a good name in the sight of God and man. Trust in the Lord with all your heart and lean not on your own understanding; in all your ways submit to Him, and he will make your paths straight. Do not be wise in your own eyes; fear the Lord and shun evil. This will bring health to your body and nourishment to your bones". ~ **Proverbs 3:1~8**

"We must pay the most careful attention, therefore, to what we have heard, so that we do not drift away. For since the message spoken through angels was binding, and every violation and disobedience received its just punishment, how shall we escape if we ignore so great a salvation? This salvation, which was first announced by the Lord, was confirmed to us by those who heard Him. God also testified to it by signs, wonders and various miracles, and by gifts of the Holy Spirit distributed according to His will". ~ **Hebrews 2:1~4**

"Humble yourselves, therefore, under God's mighty hand, that he may lift you up in due time. Cast all your anxiety on Him because he cares for you. Be alert and of sober mind. Your enemy the devil prowls around like a roaring lion looking for someone to devour. Resist Him, standing firm in the faith, because you know that the family of believers throughout the world is undergoing the same kind of sufferings. And the God of all grace, who called you to His eternal glory in Christ, after you have suffered a little while, will Himself restore you and make you strong, firm and steadfast. To Him be the power for ever and ever. Amen". ~ **1 Peter 5:6~11**

"Rejoice in the Lord always. I will say it again: Rejoice! Let your gentleness be evident to all. The Lord is near. Do not be anxious about anything, but in every situation, by prayer and petition, with thanksgiving, present your requests to God. And the peace of God, which transcends all understanding, will guard your hearts and your minds in Christ Jesus. Finally, brothers and sisters, whatever is true, whatever is noble, whatever is right, whatever is pure, whatever is lovely, whatever is admirable - if anything is excellent or praiseworthy - think about such things. Whatever you have learned or received or heard from me or seen in me - put it into practice. And the God of peace will be with you". ~ **Philippians 4:4~9**

"May the God of hope fill you with all joy and peace as you trust in Him, so that you may overflow with hope by the power of the Holy Spirit". ~ **Romans 15:13**

"For God is not a God of disorder but of peace - as in all the congregations of the Lord's people". ~ **1 Corinthians 14:33**

Prayer

Dear God,

Please calm me and bless me with love, wisdom, and understanding. Let me think of others as I make decisions for myself and my family. Let my decisions display my love and trust for You and everyone concerned. Guide my heart and spirit, keeping them in accord with Your will and my purpose. God, I thank You for wisdom, mercy, and grace. Thank You for loving me and help me to love everyone else.

In Jesus' Name.
Amen

Gina Erwin

Date: _____

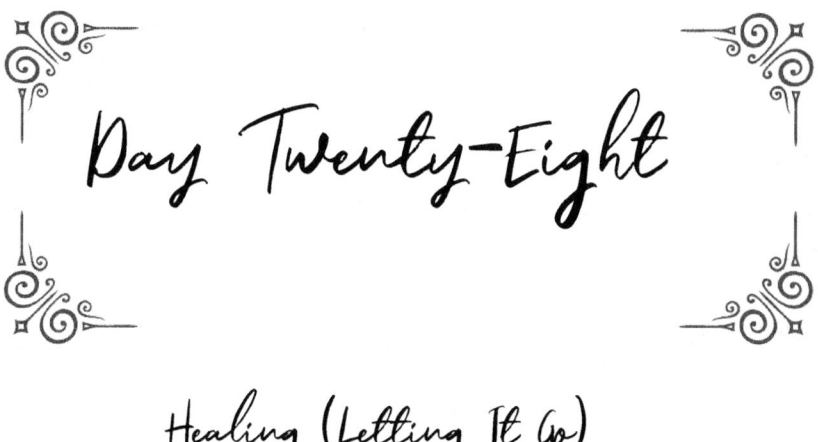

Day Twenty-Eight

Healing (Letting It Go)

I know most of you have heard the saying, "Let go and let God!". It is time for you to let go. You have acknowledged, discerned, and comprehended all aspects of the situation. You are in the process of forgiving, deciding, and healing to move forward. To heal completely and correctly, you must let it go. When you truly let something go and give it to God, you take your hands off it and stop trying to fix or handle it. You pray for God's guidance and do as His Holy Spirit moves you to do.

Letting go is one of the hardest things to do. However, it is the best thing for you, and everyone concerned. When you truly let it go, God will work it out for your good. We must learn that God manages things better than we could ever think of. When you let God have it, the weight is removed from you and you can go forward doing what God wants you to do. Pray before during and after letting go. Do not go back and try to pick it up once you give it to God. Let God have it. If you pick it back up and start messing God will not fix it because you are interfering.

Scriptures

"And we know that in all things God works for the good of those who love Him, who have been called according to His purpose". ~ **Romans 8:28**

"Come to me, all you who are weary and burdened, and I will give you rest. Take my yoke upon you and learn from me, for I am gentle and humble in heart, and you will find rest for your souls. For my yoke is easy and my burden is light". ~ **Matthew 11:28~30**

"He says, "Be still, and know that I am God; I will be exalted among the nations, I will be exalted in the earth". The Lord Almighty is with us; the God of Jacob is our fortress". ~ **Psalm 46:10~11**

"Create in me a pure heart, O God, and renew a steadfast spirit within me. Do not cast me from your presence or take your Holy Spirit from me. Restore to me the joy of your salvation and grant me a willing spirit, to sustain me". ~ **Psalm 51:10~12**

"Therefore, I tell you, do not worry about your life, what you will eat or drink; or about your body, what you will wear. Is not life more than food, and the body more than clothes? Look at the birds of the air; they do not sow or reap or store away in barns, and yet your heavenly Father feeds them. Are you not much more valuable than they? Can any one of you by worrying add a single hour to your life?" ~ **Matthew 6:25~27**

"Consider it pure joy, my brothers and sisters, whenever you face trials of many kinds, because you know that the testing of your faith produces perseverance. Let perseverance finish its work so that you may be mature and complete, not lacking anything. If any of you lacks wisdom, you should ask God, who gives generously to all without finding fault, and it will be given to you. But when you ask, you must believe and not doubt, because the one who doubts is like a wave of the sea, blown and tossed by the wind. That person should not expect to receive anything from the Lord. Such a person is double-minded and unstable in all they do". ~ **James 1:2~8**

"Blessed is the one who perseveres under trial because, having stood the test, that person will receive the crown of life that the Lord has promised to those who love Him". ~ **James 1:12**

"Don't be deceived, my dear brothers and sisters. Every good and perfect gift is from above, coming down from the Father of the heavenly lights, who does not change like shifting shadows. He chose to give us birth through the word of truth, that we might be a kind of first fruits of all he created". ~ **James 1:16~18**

"Humble yourselves, therefore, under God's mighty hand, that he may lift you up in due time. Cast all your anxiety on Him because he cares for you". ~ **1 Peter 5:6~7**

"Blessed is the nation whose God is the Lord, the people he chose for His inheritance. From heaven the Lord looks down and sees all mankind; from His dwelling place he watches all who live on earth - he who forms the hearts of all, who considers everything they do". ~ **Psalm 33:12~15**

Gina Erwin

Prayer

Dear God in Heaven,

Help me make the right decisions and let go. You are all-knowing and all-seeing. You know what is right and what must be done. Guide my steps and release me from worry. It will all work out if it is in Your hands. I do not possess the wisdom and knowledge to do anything without You. Help me let go and not try to fix it on my own. Help me give it to You and leave it with You. God thank You for all You have done and all You will continue to do in my life. Bless all those involved in this situation. Thank You for wisdom and understanding. Thank You for being You and being there for me.

In the Mighty Name of Jesus, I Pray,
Amen

Putting the Pieces Back Together After Divorce

Date: _____

_____
_____
_____
_____
_____
_____
_____
_____
_____
_____
_____
_____

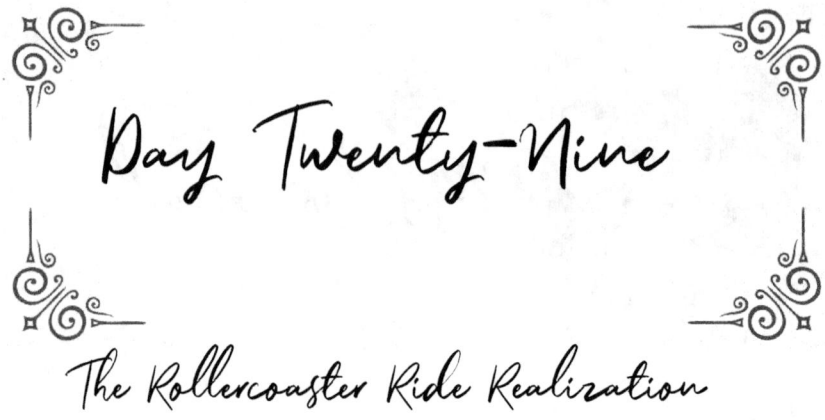

Day Twenty-Nine

The Rollercoaster Ride Realization

Rollercoaster ride? Are we going to an amusement park? No. I want you to be aware of the rollercoaster ride you will be on for a while and maybe long into the future. I consider it a rollercoaster ride because it is filled with ups and downs that come and go randomly.

Throughout your life, a song may play, a movie may be seen, a photograph may pop up, or anything may happen that will jog your memory of past times both good and bad. Whether you stay with your spouse or not, these memories are a part of your History and they have a way of coming up from time to time. I want you to be prepared and not overreact when it happens.

Sometimes I hear a song that my husband used to sing to me or that was played at my wedding and my mind automatically goes back to that moment in time. You too, have many memories that are in your brain and can surface at any time. This is okay and a part of life. Our memories are special and serve to inform us as well. When this happens and you do not like the way you are feeling, pray to God. Pray, so that these feelings and memories do not take you to a place where you do not want or need to be.

You will have good days and bad days. No matter which, pray and stay in close contact with God because He will keep you on the right path no matter how you are feeling. Enjoy the good days and if you need to cry on the bad days, cry. It is okay to cry. Tears cleanse the soul. Just be aware that memories and emotions last a lifetime and they surface when they surface.

Scriptures

"Before Isaiah had left the middle court, the word of the Lord came to Him: Go back and tell Hezekiah, the ruler of my people, This is what the Lord, the God of your father David, says: I have heard your prayer and seen your tears; I will heal you." ~ **2 Kings 20:4~5**

"I love the Lord, for he heard my voice; he heard my cry for mercy. Because he turned His ear to me, I will call on Him as long as I live. The cords of death entangled me, the anguish of the grave came over me; I was overcome by distress and sorrow. Then I called on the name of the Lord: "Lord, save me!" The Lord is gracious and righteous; our God is full of compassion. The Lord protects the unwary; when I was brought low, he saved me. Return to your rest, my soul, for the Lord has been good to you. For you, Lord, have delivered me from death, my eyes from tears, my feet from stumbling, that I may walk before the Lord in the land of the living". ~ **Psalm 116:1~9**

"Those who sow with tears will reap with songs of joy. Those who go out weeping, carrying seed to sow, will return with songs of joy, carrying sheaves with them". ~ **Psalm 126:5~6**

"He will swallow up death forever. The Sovereign Lord will wipe away the tears from all faces; he will remove His people's disgrace from all the earth. The Lord has spoken". ~ **Isaiah 25:8**

Gina Erwin

Prayer

Dear God,

Thank You for the good and bad times. Thank You for the lessons learned. God guide me as memories come and go. Help me to see the importance in them and avoid any negativity attached to them. Wipe my tears and allow the negativity to flow away from me in my tears. I need You always God. Stay with me in good and bad times. With You I can and will overcome.

In Jesus Name,
Amen

Putting the Pieces Back Together After Divorce

Date: _____

_____
_____
_____
_____
_____
_____
_____
_____
_____
_____
_____
_____

Day Thirty

Moving Forward

Moving forward, you must continue to pray, study the bible ~ God's word, and focus on the purpose and plans God has for your life. Reach out and help others, showing love to all. Forgive when someone hurts or harms you. Trust God and let Him guide you through every situation. Proclaim His Name and tell others how God has blessed and kept you in times of hardship and trouble. Focus on the good and not the bad. Thank God for all things. Remember to look for the lesson in all things and use them to help others and glorify God.

If you are still having difficulties with any area of the book, go back and reread it. If you need to go back to the beginning and start the book over, then do so. Focus on what the scriptures are telling and showing you. Be still and listen for God's guidance. When you draw close to Him, He will guide and protect you.

Whatever decisions you have made, be sure they are in accordance with God. Whatever decisions you still must make, trust God to guide you. Do everything out of love and not negativity.

God will continue to propel you forward and make your paths straight. Keep Him first and all other things will come, and you will be prosperous moving forward.

Putting the Pieces Back Together After Divorce

Scriptures

"My son, do not forget my teaching, but keep my commands in your heart, for they will prolong your life many years and bring you peace and prosperity. Let love and faithfulness never leave you; bind them around your neck, write them on the tablet of your heart. Then you will win favor and a good name in the sight of God and man. Trust in the Lord with all your heart and lean not on your own understanding; in all your ways submit to Him, and he will make your paths straight". ~ **Proverbs 3:1~6**

"Do you not know? Have you not heard? The Lord is the everlasting God, the Creator of the ends of the earth. He will not grow tired or weary, and His understanding no one can fathom. He gives strength to the weary and increases the power of the weak. Even youths grow tired and weary, and young men stumble and fall; but those who hope in the Lord will renew their strength. They will soar on wings like eagles; they will run and not grow weary; they will walk and not be faint". ~ **Isaiah 40:28~31**

"I will exalt you, Lord, for you lifted me out of the depths and did not let my enemies gloat over me. Lord my God, I called to you for help, and you healed me. You, Lord, brought me up from the realm of the dead; you spared me from going down to the pit. Sing the praises of the Lord, you His faithful people; praise His holy name. For His anger lasts only a moment, but His favor lasts a lifetime; weeping may stay for the night, but rejoicing comes in the morning. When I felt secure, I said, "I will never be shaken". Lord, when you favored me, you made my royal mountain stand firm; but when you hid your face, I was dismayed. To you, Lord, I called; to the Lord I cried for mercy: "What is gained if I am silenced, if I go down to the pit? Will the dust praise you? Will it proclaim your faithfulness? Hear, Lord, and be merciful to me; Lord, be my help". You turned my wailing into dancing; you removed my sackcloth and clothed me with joy, that my heart may sing your praises and not be silent. Lord my God, I will praise you forever". ~ **Psalm 30**

"Do your best to present yourself to God as one approved, a worker who does not need to be ashamed and who correctly handles the word of truth". ~ **2 Timothy 2:15**

"No king is saved by the size of His army, no warrior escapes by His great strength. A horse is a vain hope for deliverance; despite all its great strength it cannot save. But the eyes of the Lord are on those who fear Him, on those whose hope is in His unfailing love, to deliver them from death and keep them alive in famine. We wait in hope for the Lord; he is our help and our shield. In Him our hearts rejoice, for we trust in His holy name. May your unfailing love be with us, Lord, even as we put our hope in you". ~ **Psalm 33:16~22**

"In fact, everyone who wants to live a Godly life in Christ Jesus will be persecuted, while evildoers and impostors will go from bad to worse, deceiving and being deceived. But as for you, continue in what you have learned and have become convinced of, because you know those from whom you learned it, and how from infancy you have known the Holy Scriptures, which are able to make you wise for salvation through faith in Christ Jesus. All Scripture is God-breathed and is useful for teaching, rebuking, correcting, and training in righteousness, so that the servant of God[a] may be thoroughly equipped for every good work". ~ **2 Timothy 3:12~17**

"But since we belong to the day, let us be sober, putting on faith and love as a breastplate, and the hope of salvation as a helmet. For God did not appoint us to suffer wrath but to receive salvation through our Lord Jesus Christ. He died for us so that, whether we are awake or asleep, we may live together with Him. Therefore encourage one another and build each other up, just as in fact you are doing. Now we ask you, brothers and sisters, to acknowledge those who work hard among you, who care for you in the Lord and who admonish you. Hold them in the highest regard in love because of their work. Live in peace with each other. And we urge you, brothers, and sisters, warn those who are idle and disruptive, encourage the disheartened, help the weak, be patient with everyone. Make sure that nobody pays back wrong for wrong, but always strive to do what is good for each other and for everyone else. Rejoice always, pray continually, give thanks in all circumstances; for this is God's will for you in Christ Jesus. Do not quench the Spirit. Do not treat prophecies with contempt but test them all; hold on to what is good, reject every kind of evil. May God Himself, the God of peace, sanctify you through and through. May your whole spirit, soul and body be kept blameless at the coming of our Lord Jesus Christ. The one who calls you is faithful, and he will do it. Brothers and sisters, pray for us. Greet all God's people with a holy kiss. I charge you before the Lord to have this letter read to all the brothers and sisters. The grace of our Lord Jesus Christ be with you". ~ **1 Thessalonians 5:8~28**

"Finally, be strong in the Lord and in His mighty power. Put on the full armor of God, so that you can take your stand against the devil's schemes. For our struggle is not against flesh and blood, but against the rulers, against the authorities, against the powers of this dark world and against the spiritual forces of evil in the heavenly realms. Therefore, put on the full armor of God, so that when the day of evil comes, you may be able to stand your ground, and after you have done everything, to stand. Stand firm then, with the belt of truth buckled around your waist, with the breastplate of righteousness in place, and with your feet fitted with the readiness that comes from the gospel of peace. In addition to all this, take up the shield of faith, with which you can extinguish all the flaming arrows of the evil one. Take the helmet of salvation and the sword of the Spirit, which is the word of God. And pray in the Spirit on all occasions with all kinds of prayers and requests. With this in mind, be alert and always keep on praying for all the Lord's people". ~ **Ephesians 6:10~18**

"Therefore, we do not lose heart. Though outwardly we are wasting away, yet inwardly we are being renewed day by day. For our light and momentary troubles are achieving for us an eternal glory that far outweighs them all. So, we fix our eyes not on what is seen, but on what is unseen, since what is seen is temporary, but what is unseen is eternal". ~ **2 Corinthians 4:16~18**

"Here is a trustworthy saying that deserves full acceptance: Christ Jesus came into the world to save sinners - of whom I am the worst. But for that very reason I was shown mercy so that in me, the worst of sinners, Christ Jesus might display His immense patience as an example for those who would believe in Him and receive eternal life. Now to the King eternal, immortal, invisible, the only God, be honor and glory for ever and ever. Amen". ~ **1 Timothy 1:15~17**

Putting the Pieces Back Together After Divorce

Prayer

Father in Heaven,

Thank You for helping me through this and protecting me from being overtaken by emotions and feelings. Thank You for Your love, kindness, mercy, forgiveness, grace, wisdom, and understanding. Guide me forward and keep me focused on You. Love and forgive all those who brought hurt and harm to me and my spirit. Show me what You want me to do and how You want me to do it. Be my guide, my rock, and my strength. Surround me with individuals that focus on You and Your will. Allow me to move forward in love and help all who cross my path in any way I can. Allow me to glorify and praise Your Name always. Thank You, God. I love You.

In the Mighty Name of Jesus,
Amen

My Journal

Date: _____

Day Thirty-one

Turning Tests into Testimonies & Pain into Purpose

You are probably wondering how you can take this painful situation and make something good come of it. You can. First you need to address your passion. What do you enjoy doing? What activities bring you joy and peace? Do you enjoy writing, speaking, counseling others, praying, entertaining, cooking, baking, singing, or anything else? If you enjoy writing, you can author books, songs, memoirs, or articles. If you enjoy speaking, you can speak to women. If you enjoy counseling, you can get certified and counsel. If you enjoy entertaining, you can start a weekly or monthly event. If you enjoy cooking or baking, you can prepare meals or desserts for weekly or monthly events and create a peaceful, enjoyable, atmosphere for women to open up and talk. If you enjoy singing, you can sing. Whatever you enjoy can be used to reach out to and uplift other women who have gone through adultery and other issues you have encountered. Weekly or monthly functions that allow women to talk and communicate openly can be used by entertaining, cooking, baking, and even singing. You can write a blog, column, newsletter, books, and articles that will help other women. You can start a prayer group in person or online. Whatever your talent and passion, you can use it to help others and spread the good news about God and how He will help women in their situations and with their issues.

Authoring this book was a form of therapy for me and a way to reach out to other women dealing with some of the same issues. You never know who your story will touch and help. One word from you may be the one thing that some other women needs to hear. I thank God for my friend who had experienced some of the things I was going through and talked to me about them. Her testimony and words help me to look to God and think before I made any decisions.

God is love and He wants us to love each other. When you love others, you seek ways to help them when they are in need and/or hurting. Everyone cannot afford counseling, so just being able to hear the testimonies of other women may be the help they need.

Everything happens for a reason. Look at the cup as half full and not half empty. Ask yourself, "What did I learn from this experience?" and "How can I help others with what I experienced and now know?". Use your experiences to help, assist, uplift, and empower others. It just does not have to be with adultery. It can be with any topic you have encountered and successfully dealt with in your life.

Using your experiences to help and empower others will glorify God and allow you to show others how God got you through. It will also show God you love Him and others. Showing love is the greatest commandment and this is truly a way to do so. Remember whichever path you choose, pray, and ask God for the guidance and wisdom to help those who come across your path.

Scriptures

"There is a time for everything, and a season for every activity under the heavens: a time to be born and a time to die, a time to plant and a time to uproot, a time to kill and a time to heal, a time to tear down and a time to build, a time to weep and a time to laugh, a time to mourn and a time to dance, a time to scatter stones and a time to gather them, a time to embrace and a time to refrain from embracing, a time to search and a time to give up, a time to keep and a time to throw away, a time to tear and a time to mend, a time to be silent and a time to speak, a time to love and a time to hate, a time for war and a time for peace." ~ **Ecclesiastes 3:1~8**

"I will extol the Lord at all times; His praise will always be on my lips. I will glory in the Lord; let the afflicted hear and rejoice. Glorify the Lord with me; let us exalt His name together. I sought the Lord, and he answered me; he delivered me from all my fears. Those who look to Him are radiant; their faces are never covered with shame. This poor man called, and the Lord heard Him; he saved Him out of all His troubles. The angel of the Lord encamps around those who fear Him, and he delivers them. Taste and see that the Lord is good; blessed is the one who takes refuge in Him. Fear the Lord, you His holy people, for those who fear Him lack nothing. The lions may grow weak and hungry, but those who seek the Lord lack no good thing. Come, my children, listen to me; I will teach you the fear of the Lord. Whoever of you loves life and desires to see many good days, keep your tongue from evil and your lips from telling lies. Turn from evil and do good; seek peace and pursue it. The eyes of the Lord are on the righteous, and His ears are attentive to their cry; but the face of the Lord is against those who do evil, to blot out their name from the earth. The righteous cry out, and the Lord hears them; he delivers them from all their troubles. The Lord is close to the brokenhearted and saves those who are crushed in spirit. The righteous person may have many troubles, but the Lord delivers Him from them all; he protects all His bones, not one of them will be broken. Evil will slay the wicked; the foes of the righteous will be condemned. The Lord will rescue His servants; no one who takes refuge in Him will be condemned". ~ **Psalm 34**

"Trust in the Lord and do good; dwell in the land and enjoy safe pasture. Take delight in the Lord, and he will give you the desires of your heart. Commit your way to the Lord; trust in Him and he will do this: He will make your righteous reward shine like the dawn, your vindication like the noonday sun". ~ **Psalm 37:3~6**

"God "will repay each person according to what they have done". To those who by persistence in doing good seek glory, honor, and immortality, he will give eternal life". ~ **Romans 2:6~7**

"I have the right to do anything", you say—but not everything is beneficial. "I have the right to do anything"—but not everything is constructive. No one should seek their own good, but the good of others". ~ **1 Corinthians 10:23~24**

"This is how we know what love is: Jesus Christ laid down His life for us. And we ought to lay down our lives for our brothers and sisters. If anyone has material possessions and sees a brother or sister in need but has no pity on them, how can the love of God be in that person? Dear children, let us not love with words or speech but with actions and in truth". ~ **1 John 3:16~18**

"We who are strong ought to bear with the failings of the weak and not to please ourselves. Each of us should please our neighbors for their good, to build them up. For even Christ did not please Himself but, as it is written: "The insults of those who insult you have fallen on me". For everything that was written in the past was written to teach us, so that through the endurance taught in the Scriptures and the encouragement they provide we might have hope.

May the God who gives endurance and encouragement give you the same attitude of mind toward each other that Christ Jesus had, so that with one mind and one voice you may glorify the God and Father of our Lord Jesus Christ." ~ **Romans 15:1~6**

Gina Erwin

Prayer

My Father in Heaven,

Thank You for this process and all that it has taught me. Help to use this situation to reach out to others and help them in love. Allow me to use this situation to show others of Your loving kindness. You are great and with You I can do remarkable things in Your Name. I love and need You God, always. Turn my tests into testimonies and my pain into a passion to fulfill the purpose You have set for me. Allow me to fulfill that purpose and bring great praise and glory to Your Name. Thank You, God!

In Jesus' Mighty Name,
Amen

Putting the Pieces Back Together After Divorce

Date: _____

_____
_____
_____
_____
_____
_____
_____
_____
_____
_____
_____
_____

Conclusion

Adultery has occurred and you are getting through it with the help of God, family, and friends. I pray this book has helped you as well. Adultery occurs daily and it hurts. Why does it hurt? Because it affects the core of your being, your heart. This is the place God lives. You allow certain people into your heart expecting for them to love you back in return. The Bible, God's Word explains that is what real love is.

> "Love is patient, love is kind. It does not envy, it does not boast, it is not proud. It does not dishonor others, it is not self-seeking, it is not easily angered, it keeps no record of wrongs. Love does not delight in evil but rejoices with the truth. It always protects, always trusts, always hopes, always perseveres. Love never fails".
> ~ 1 Corinthians 13: 4-8

Due to the imperfect state of humanity and the world, we all love differently. No one absolutely loves unconditionally like God does. We cannot because we are imperfect. However, do not let that stop you from doing your best to love God, yourself, and others.

One of the many lessons I learned from my experience with adultery was how powerful and forgiving God's love truly is. After everything had been said and done, I still loved my husband despite what he did and how bad it hurt. I could not understand why or even how I could still love Him. This taught me how God loves us. We fall short of pleasing God and hurt Him every day of our lives. We do not necessarily do it on purpose, but we do. Yet, God does not stop loving us. He continues to love us and desires for us to get ourselves back on track and live according to His will and purpose. So, even when someone hurts you and you still love that person, know that you truly love that person as God loves us and desires for us to love others. Through the pain I learned how God loves us all even when we do not deserve it.

I also learned that I do not need a man to love me to validate who I am or my worthiness of love. God loves me and that is enough. If I never find love again, I know I did experience it for a moment in my life and for that I will always be grateful. If I do find love again, I have learned a lot about God and myself to give my all to the relationship. I do know that nothing is perfect except for God and that it will take God, communication, trust, and unconditional love on both of our parts to make it work.

Become the woman God has destined you to be and He will bless you with the man that is right for you and chosen by Him. Patience is a virtue and exercising it will bless you. Do not let this experience stop you in your tracks or keep you from loving again. Use this experience to help you love God and yourself, strengthen you, teach you, and motivate you into your purpose. Turn your tests into testimonies, your trials into teachings, your tribulations into tell-all's, and your pain into your purpose.

Following *'the Bible Verse that Inspired the Book'*, there is an affirmation that I pray each of you say out loud and believe it as you read it. Read it every day until it is truly incorporated into your heart and it motivates you move forward in your purpose.

You will heal and you will be prosperous if you trust God and keep Him first in all you do. You are a daughter of the King and this too shall pass.

MAY GOD BLESS YOU!
I pray Blessings over you, your life, and your Family!

Gina Erwin

Bible Verse that Inspired the Book

"Furious with rage, Nebuchadnezzar summoned Shadrach, Meshach and Abednego. So, these men were brought before the king, and Nebuchadnezzar said to them, "Is it true, Shadrach, Meshach and Abednego, that you do not serve my Gods or worship the image of gold I have set up? Now when you hear the sound of the horn, flute, zither, lyre, harp, pipe and all kinds of music, if you are ready to fall down and worship the image I made, very good. But if you do not worship it, you will be thrown immediately into a blazing furnace. Then what God will be able to rescue you from my hand?" Shadrach, Meshach and Abednego replied to Him, "King Nebuchadnezzar, we do not need to defend ourselves before you in this matter. If we are thrown into the blazing furnace, the God we serve is able to deliver us from it, and he will deliver us[c] from Your Majesty's hand. But even if he does not, we want you to know, Your Majesty, that we will not serve your Gods or worship the image of gold you have set up". Then Nebuchadnezzar was furious with Shadrach, Meshach and Abednego, and His attitude toward them changed. He ordered the furnace heated seven times hotter than usual and commanded some of the strongest soldiers in His army to tie up Shadrach, Meshach and Abednego and throw them into the blazing furnace. So, these men, wearing their robes, trousers, turbans, and other clothes, were bound, and thrown into the blazing furnace. The king's command was so urgent and the furnace so hot that the flames of the fire killed the soldiers who took up Shadrach, Meshach and Abednego, and these three men, firmly tied, fell into the blazing furnace. Then King Nebuchadnezzar leaped to His feet in amazement and asked His advisers, "Weren't there three men that we tied up and threw into the fire?" They

replied, "Certainly, Your Majesty". He said, "Look! I see four men walking around in the fire, unbound and unharmed, and the fourth looks like a son of the Gods". Nebuchadnezzar then approached the opening of the blazing furnace and shouted, "Shadrach, Meshach and Abednego, servants of the Most High God, come out! Come here!" So, Shadrach, Meshach and Abednego came out of the fire, and the satraps, prefects, governors, and royal advisers crowded around them. They saw that the fire had not harmed their bodies, nor was a hair of their heads singed; their robes were not scorched, and there was no smell of fire on them. Then Nebuchadnezzar said, "Praise be to the God of Shadrach, Meshach, and Abednego, who has sent His angel and rescued His servants! They trusted in Him and defied the king's command and were willing to give up their lives rather than serve or worship any God except their own God. Therefore, I decree that the people of any nation or language who say anything against the God of Shadrach, Meshach and Abednego be cut into pieces and their houses be turned into piles of rubble, for no other God can save in this way." Then the king promoted Shadrach, Meshach, and Abednego in the
province of Babylon". ~ Daniel 3:13~30

God will protect and keep you if you place Him first and allow nothing and no one to take your worship and your focus away from Him.

Gina Erwin

Affirmation Statement

I am special. I am a daughter of the King. I have a purpose. God loves me. He wants the best for me. He sees the best in me even if I cannot see it.

My personal situation is affecting me. However, it is not defining who I am, where I am going or who I will become. That is God's plan and my choice.

My glass is half full, not half empty. I will use the bad to reinforce the good and the negative to reinforce the positive.

From this day forward, I will move forward, walking in the purpose and plan God has for me and my life's journey. With God by my side I can do anything and do it well.

Today is the first day of the rest of my life, my great Godly life. I will fulfill God's plan for me. I will be the virtuous woman God destined me to be.

Amen! Amen! Amen!

About the Author

Gina is a native New Yorker and former teacher and secretary. She moved to North Carolina in 1989 and has worked extensively in the church as a Sunday school teacher, Pastor's Assistant, church secretary and other capacities. Gina has attained her BS in Business Administration with a concentration in Technical Communication (2016) and her Master's in Business (MLBA) at Oral Roberts University with a Christian Leadership certification (2018). She is currently working on her PhD in Christian Leadership and Ministry at Liberty University.

Gina's current capacity is that of mother, author, personal assistant, Senior Director and Prayer Leader at Divorce Recovery Advocates Working for Women, Senior Publishing Advocate and assistant to the Editor and Chief of IGM Productions LLC. She is a mother of three beautiful children, a son and two daughters and has two grandchildren. They are her motivation and inspiration. As an adolescent, Gina wrote her first picture book that was published in-house through the New York

Home Instruction Library. She loves writing and her greatest hope is that her writing empowers and aids others through their personal trials in life.

"Putting the Pieces Back Together After Adultery" is Gina first book as an adult and her stepping out on faith in God. As someone who has been on both sides of adultery, Gina prays that her tests and trials can aid others going through some of the same things. She is also currently working on her next book, "Spirit vs. Flesh: The Battle Within".

Contact Gina here;

authorizeddaughterofGod@gmail.com

www.facebook.com/GinaAuthorizedDaughterOfGOD

Putting the Pieces Back Together After Divorce

Coming Soon from Gina Erwin

Spirit vs. Flesh: The Battle Within

The Butterfly Effect

www.ingramcontent.com/pod-product-compliance
Lightning Source LLC
LaVergne TN
LVHW051520070426
835507LV00023B/3212